Sanatan Dharma - The power of boundless love

by
Diptiman Gaurahari das
& Diptimayi Vishnupriya devi dasi

Founders of 'The Gaudiya Treasures of Bengal'
(www.thegaudiyatreasuresofbengal.com)

Copyright © 2020 by Dwaipayan De (Diptiman Gaurahari das)
All rights reserved.

Dedication

*Nama om vishnu-padaya Krishna-preshthaya
bhu-tale
Srimate Jayapataka Svamin iti namine
Nama acharya Padaya, Nitai Kripa Pradayine*

Website - www.thegaudiyatreasuresofbengal.com

Gaur Katha Dhama-udaya, Nagara Grama Tarine

We dedicate this book and its contents to our beloved spiritual master, HH Jayapataka Swami Guru Maharaja, whose blessings have empowered us ineligible fools to tread the path of bhakti. His Holiness has shown us how to love and engage oneself completely in the service of Sri Krishna. An intimate associate of the Lord, he relentlessly executes his great services, not caring a bit for his advanced age or his difficult physical condition. His exemplary mood and instructions have been instrumental in us sustaining our spiritual lives. We hanker for his blessings and hope he accepts the offerings of us insignificant servants.

Website - www.thegaudiyatreasuresofbengal.com

About the Author

Diptiman Gaurahari das (Dwaipayan De) is employed as a senior software engineer in a reputed MNC. Diptimayi Vishnupriya devi dasi (Debdatta De) serves as a dutiful homemaker. They are also the founders of www.thegaudiyatreasuresofbengal.com, a very popular website dedicated to the service of the Supreme Lord and His devotees. Diptiman Gaurahari das and Diptimayi Vishnupriya devi dasi are actively engaged in teaching the glories of Sanatan Dharma worldwide. Their authored books and contribution in this field have been well received and appreciated by the practitioners of Sanatan Dharma all over the world.

Website - www.thegaudiyatreasuresofbengal.com

Disclaimer

1. Although the author and publisher have made every effort to ensure that the information in this book was correct at press time, the author and publisher do not assume and hereby disclaim any liability to any party for any loss, damage, or disruption caused by errors or omissions, whether such errors or omissions result from negligence, accident, or any other cause.

2. This book is not intended as a substitute for the medical advice of physicians. The reader should regularly consult a physician in matters relating to his/her health and particularly with respect to any symptoms that may require diagnosis or medical attention.

3. Any views or opinions provided in this book are not intended to malign any religion, ethnic group, club, organization, company, ideology, individual, anyone or anything. All content provided in this book is for informational purposes only.

Website - www.thegaudiyatreasuresofbengal.com

The author and publisher of this book make no representations as to the accuracy or completeness of any information on this book or found by following any link contained in this book.

Website - www.thegaudiyatreasuresofbengal.com

Table of Contents

Dedication	1
About the Author	3
Disclaimer	4
Table of Contents	6
Spirituality, Spiritual Knowledge and why it is important	13
Spiritual Knowledge - Are we our Bodies ?	14
Looking beyond - Is Spirituality important ?	17
The spiritual identity :	22
Spiritual Knowledge - The needs of the Soul :	23
Yoga as explained in the Bhagavad Gita	26
The Yoga ladder	28
Karma Yoga :	28
Jnana Yoga:	30
Dhyana Yoga:	32
Bhakti Yoga:	36

Website - www.thegaudiyatreasuresofbengal.com

What is Sanatan Dharma?   39

    Eternal Nature (Sanatan Dharma) vs
Temporary Nature (Naimittika Dharma)   40

    What is the 'Sanatan Dharma' of Man ?   42

    The science of Life :   46

    Misdirected service - Root cause of all evil
                                              49

    Is Sanatan Dharma Sectarian?   53

    Does Sanatan Dharma imply rejection of matter?   53

    Practicing Sanatan Dharma :   57

How old is the Indian civilization and its Sanatan Dharma?   61

    What are the Vedas ?   62

    So how old is the Indian Civilization? - Digging into the Past   65

       #2 Discovering River Saraswati   66

       #3 Ancient Hindu Temples found worldwide   67

       #4 Major Anthropology Find Reported in India   72

       #5 Tamil Brahmi Script Found in Egypt
                                              73

    Vedic Culture and today's world   74

    The Ultimate Message of the Vedas   76

The Indian Varna System   78

Website - www.thegaudiyatreasuresofbengal.com

The essence of the Indian Varna system : 79
Efficacy of the Indian Varna system (Caste system) : 83
Degradation of the Indian Varna system : 86
The fallacy of birth determining caste : Who is a brahmana? 89
Towards the perfect society – Incorporating the Varna system : 95
Sources : 98

Atheism vs Spirituality 99

Incompatibility of Matter and Spirit - Atheism vs Spirituality 101
Fallacy of Materialistic Philosophies - Atheism vs Spirituality 111
The perfect Classless Society 113
Ending notes 117

Depression and Anxiety - A Spiritual Solution 119

Root cause of Anxiety and Depression - Mistaken identity of the Self 120
"What lies behind us and what lies before us are tiny as compared to what lies within us" 123
The True Nature of the Self : 125
Does spirituality imply rejection of Matter ? 128
Reviving one's spiritual consciousness 131

Website - www.thegaudiyatreasuresofbengal.com

Bhakti Yoga and Ashtanga Yoga   134

   Types of Yoga - Superiority of Bhakti Yoga
       137

   The path of Ashtanga Yoga is full of impediments :   140

   Types of Yoga - The Yogi responds :   142

   Bhakti Yoga cannot be practiced as a dry selfish fruitive ritual :   143

27 facts of Life   146

15 Benefits of Chanting Hare Krishna Mahamantra | Glories of Hare Krishna Mahamantra   173

   #1 In this age of Kali the only means of spiritual salvation is the chanting of Krishna's holy name and glories (Sri-Krishna-Kirtana). No other activity surpasses the effectiveness of this.   174

   #2 Chanting the Holy name of Lord Hari destroys all sins   175

   #3 Religious rites and vows are insignificant in comparison to chanting the Holy Name of Hari   177

   #4 One who chants the holy name of Lord Hari attains Vaikuntha   179

   #5 Chanting absolves sins of the past as well as sins that are yet to fructify   181

   #6 The Holy name cures all diseases   183

Website - www.thegaudiyatreasuresofbengal.com

#7 The Holy Name transforms the greatest sinners into the most glorious saints — 184

#8 Chanting the Holy name dispels fear and punishments — 185

#9 Chanting the Holy name of Lord Hari with faith counteracts the adverse ill-effects of Kali Yuga — 187

#10 Chanting the Holy name of Lord Hari is superior to the study of all 4 Vedas — 188

#11 The Holy name of Krishna is superior to the holy names of 'Vishnu' and 'Rama' — 190

#12 Chanting of the Holy Name of Lord Hari is superior to any pilgrimage — 193

#14 Chanting the Holy Name is superior to the practice of Sankhya and Ashtanga Yoga — 196

#15 Lord Krishna and His holy name is non-different — 198

How to Chant the Hare Krishna Mahamantra ? — 199

Meaning of Hare Krishna Mahamantra | Glories of the Hare Krishna Mahamantra — 203

The Twenty-six Qualities of a devotee — 205

Devotee of Lord Krishna | Power of devotee association — 236

Website - www.thegaudiyatreasuresofbengal.com

Pastimes from various revealed scriptures that exhibit the importance of associating with a devotee of the Supreme Lord (Sri Krishna) and avoiding the association of Non-devotees 241

Receiving the association of devotees is an outcome of causeless mercy 248

Chaitanya Mahaprabhu - Biography, Teachings & the Hare Krishna Movement 252

Sri Chaitanya Mahaprabhu - External reasons for His advent: 256

Confidential Reasons for Sri Chaitanya Mahaprabhu's appearance: 259

The dire situation of India before Sri Chaitanya Mahaprabhu had appeared in this world: 262

Celestial pastimes - Lord Krishna's confidential revelations to Narada Muni : 267

Biography of Chaitanya Mahaprabhu - In a nutshell : 274

Lord Chaitanya's Teachings in a Nutshell : 278

Chaitanya Mahaprabhu's causeless mercy : 282

Gauranga Mora Dharma (Gauranga is my 'dharma') 288

Composed by Srila Narahari Sarkara Thakura 288

Website - www.thegaudiyatreasuresofbengal.com

(Narahari Sarkara's Exclusive devotion unto Lord Chaitanya's lotus feet)   288

On a closing Note   293

Spirituality, Spiritual Knowledge and why it is important

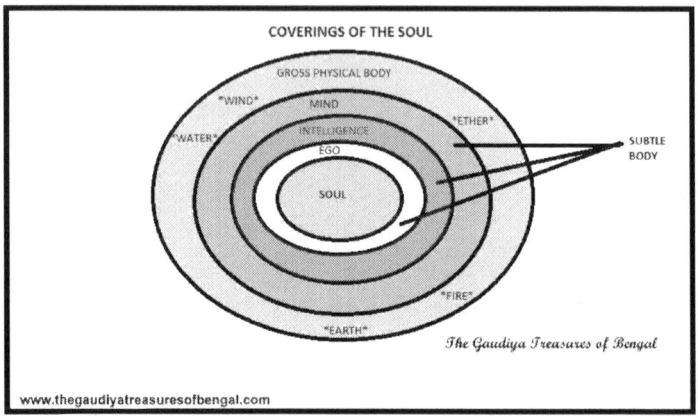

So, what is the meaning of spirituality ?

The English Dictionary defines the word "spiritual" as "Relating to or affecting the human spirit or soul as opposed to material or physical things".

Now before we delve deeper into this topic, it is essential for all of us to understand as to who we actually are? The answer to this question will help us make sense of life, in the first place, and lead us to the gradual understanding of what truly is the goal of it. In other words, the more we discuss and brainstorm on our own identity, the more clarity it shall provide to logically deduce as to what we are essentially searching for.

Spiritual Knowledge - Are we our Bodies ?

For instance, according to one popular school of thought, human beings and in fact all living beings, are nothing but a lump of flesh and blood. They argue that our activities of thinking, willing and feeling arise out of complex interactions between matter. However, we are practically yet to conceive a robot in any of our science labs, that successfully demonstrates any symptoms of creativity, inspiration or love - the elementary functions of our conscious selves. So though there is no proof to this theory, it is still nonetheless a theory, and is widely accepted and endorsed by many.

It is worthwhile mentioning over here, that a cell, which is the basic constituent of a human body, has a definite life span, and once a

Website - www.thegaudiyatreasuresofbengal.com

particular cell dies, it is replaced by another. In this way, it is believed that over a span of 7 years, all the cells that constitute the physical body of a person, are completely replaced by the new ones. So in effect, a person receives a new body every 7 years. Now if someone identifies himself with his own body, then he should be considered dead in the next seven years, as he gets physically replaced, or should we say, it is he who is completely replaced. Hence going by this chain of logic, a person should be considered a completely different individual, after a span of seven years. And the new individual, seven years older, would be a different person with different sets of qualities, nature, acumen and consciousness who would have nothing to do with the person who he had just replaced. Going further on this, a person shouldn't be sentenced for any crime, for more than seven years, as it would implicate that a different individual would have to suffer for the misdeeds he has not committed (it was committed by someone he has replaced). Another implication of this philosophy, might be the inclusion of an expiry date of seven years ,to the academic degrees. So Doctors, engineers, singers,etc need to prove their qualification

Website - www.thegaudiyatreasuresofbengal.com

periodically at a gap of seven years, as the new person might not be born as qualified as the person he had just replaced.

As strange as these might seem, it is exactly the kind of scenario we would have in our hands, if we were our bodies. I hope after deeply considering the above points, we now realize that we are not just a lump of flesh and blood, that our physical bodies are made up of. Instead, our identity remains elsewhere, far subtler than the gross material covering that encapsulates us.

So just to summarize the point that we were trying to drive home - We possess our bodies, that are made up of gross matter, but we are not our bodies. We see through our eyes ; but we are not our eyes. We remain constant, unchanged and living in the midst of the various changes that keep occurring to this material world and the body of matter that we so dearly possess.

So, where does our identity actually lie ? Who really are we ?
How to explain the consciousness of a person, in certain cases, who is lying unconscious in a state of coma ? How to explain past life

Website - www.thegaudiyatreasuresofbengal.com

memories ? How to explain OBEs (out of body experiences) or NDEs (Near Death experiences). One who's interested to get a list of these cases, can look up a very well-known book called 'Into the Unknown' published by the Reader's Digest in 1981. So, now if we are ready to look beyond this world of dead matter, let us try to dig in a bit further.

Looking beyond - Is Spirituality important ?

The Vedic literatures, which are the oldest man-written scriptures present in this world, give us some much needed insight on this subject. The Vedic scriptures, composed mainly in sanskrit, and which encompasses a huge volume of texts and manuscripts, provide a detailed analysis and a first hand experience of significant historical events, with a purpose to teach us the science of life. The vedic culture is still prevalent in certain parts of India even today, where the daily lifestyle of people and their values are in harmony with the conclusions of the vedas.

The first aphorism of the Vedanta Sutra (that reveals the method to understand the Vedic knowledge) , states *'athato brahma jijnasa'* - Now one should inquire about Brahman - The absolute truth, the transcendental, spiritual nature.

According to the Vedas, human life is very precious, for it is in this human birth that one can enquire into the ultimate truth, the reality and purpose of one's existence. We would like to hence congratulate you because you are interested in investigating the details of subjects, whose very discussion makes our lives meaningful and worthy.

The knowledge enunciated by the vedic scriptures is often referred to as Sanatan Dharma, or eternal truth - that which is universal, non-sectarian, and does not change with the effects of time,place and circumstance.

The Vedas teach us that not only humans but all living beings are essentially spirit souls.

These spiritual entities are entrapped within a body made of gross and subtle matter. The gross covering which constitutes the external physical body,consists of gross material elements like - earth ,water, fire, wind and ether. Underneath this gross body lies a subtle covering consisting of subtle elements - the mind, intelligence and ego with the intelligence being subtler than the mind, and ego being the subtlest.

Mind, Intelligence and Ego :

We all do experience the interaction of these gross and subtle entities in our day to day life to a certain extent. The senses, made up of the gross elements, help us to interact with the external world. The mind, the storehouse of the thoughts and emotions, directs the action of the senses. The intelligence, being even subtler, can exercise its power of discretion, to control the mind. Whereas the ego, defines our sense of identity, from which stems our intelligence and subsequently its discretionary powers.

For example, say, you are playing a soccer match. It is the final match of a prestigious tournament, a match in which your team depends on your skills a lot. Now suppose you face a harsh tackle, and you end up getting injured after which you can hardly walk, anymore. The gross body is clearly not in the best of shapes anymore to continue with the game, but it cannot take the decision on its own. So it looks up to the mind for a direction. The emotional mind understands that you are in a lot of pain and so decides to quit the game. But then your intelligence steps in. It logically proves to your mind, that if you quit at this stage, the team will practically be helpless. And it is afterall the final match of the tournament, and only a few more minutes are left to play. So it is wise to continue playing with the injury, as with you on the field, the team has a better chance of winning.

Similar interactions occur with students before their exams. The mind gets tired of studying for long hours and almost always wants to take a break and enjoy - maybe by watching Tv or some movies. But, good students, having strong intelligence control the demands of their minds, and continue studying, keeping in view the bigger picture.

Hence we find that the subtler the element the stronger it is; the greater is its power to control.

Thus intelligence is stronger than the mind, which in turn is stronger than the senses.

The ego comes into the picture, giving us the identity of who we think we are. It is the subtlest layer of our coverings and is the key factor which determines the kind of logic the Intelligence applies and the decisions it subsequently makes.

For example, if a person considers, life to be nothing but a combination of chemicals (dead matter), then he might not hesitate to cheat or even kill, a fellow human being for his own selfish interests - for there is no harm in this (as per his logic), as the other person he is cheating/murdering is also just a lump of chemicals. He might as well conclude that his actions are no different to just another chemical reaction.

A selfish person, who considers material consumption to be the ultimate goal of life, might disregard the interests of others, or their well-being while conducting his own business.

On the other hand, a soldier, who considers his duty above all else, might quite readily agree to

Website - www.thegaudiyatreasuresofbengal.com

sacrifice his own life, for the protection of his countrymen.

So it all depends on how we actually visualize ourselves, to be who we are, and this is what which constitutes our ego.

The spiritual identity :

So we see that though we can sometimes practically experience and feel the presence of our body, mind, intelligence and ego, we are hardly aware of our spiritual identity. According to the vedas, the real goal of life, is to realize that we are neither our body, mind,intelligence nor should we identify ourselves with any false ego. Instead, we have to understand that we are actually spirit souls and have nothing to do with this temporary, ever changing world of matter which is characterised by birth, disease, old age and death.The soul is eternal, and ever existing. The soul can neither be cut with a sword, nor moistened with water or be burnt with fire. At the time of death, just as a person puts on new garments, giving up old ones, similarly, the soul accepts new material bodies, giving up the old

Website - www.thegaudiyatreasuresofbengal.com

and useless ones. The objective of our lives should be to align our ego (true ego) to our spiritual identity and utilize the body, mind and intelligence to focus upon and nourish our actual needs (the needs of the soul).

Spiritual Knowledge - The needs of the Soul :

We need to understand that though polishing the cage is important, feeding the bird kept inside the cage is of utmost priority. We need to realize that though the brand of the car is important, it is worth its value only if it serves in reaching the destination in time.

Similarly, the body, mind and intellect is important as long it serves in fulfilling the desires of the soul. Such a harmonized body, mind or intelligence is the greatest boon one can possess. Instead, if they only serve to distract one from achieving his/her spiritual ends, they can become the greatest curse. The overall objective is to align and harmonize the functionings of the gross and subtle body, with spiritual realities.

Website - www.thegaudiyatreasuresofbengal.com

If one studies the Vedic science deeply, one comes to realize the real cravings of the soul. The soul craves for one thing, and one thing only - love. The soul is always searching to re-establish the loving relationship it once possessed with God, who is the Supersoul.

And the role of spirituality is to revive this deep dormant relationship between the soul and the supersoul. This process of uniting the soul and the supersoul is also known as Yoga.

If we study the world around us deeply, we would not find anyone who is not serving someone else. The father serves the son, the son serves his father, the wife serves his husband, the doctor serves his patients, the king serves his subjects, and so on. If someone has no one to serve, then he/she keeps a pet in his/her house and serves it. Thus, all of us are bound to serve, because by nature, the soul is a servant of the Lord, and service is a natural characteristic of the soul. The service attitude that the soul possesses towards the supersoul, is not based on any obligation, but is instead built on a foundation of a loving relationship.

Website - www.thegaudiyatreasuresofbengal.com

But the living entities, due to the intoxicating influence of the grandeur of matter, are forgetful of their original spiritual identities. And due to a lack of awareness, they generally end up identifying themselves with either one of the gross or subtle material coverings, that leads to a puffed up false ego. Such a misguided person, then attempts to rediscover the loving relationship it once possessed with the Supreme Lord, within the purview of matter, and thus gets entangled with material possessions. But in the process, neither he gets satisfied, nor the person/s he is serving gets fully satisfied- due to the misdirected nature of such service, which should be directed towards the Supreme Lord instead.

The relationships that we have with each other in this world should be thus based on appreciating our true spiritual identities and be motivated with a spirit of helping one another meet the needs of our soul.

Website - www.thegaudiyatreasuresofbengal.com

Yoga as explained in the Bhagavad Gita

What is Yoga? What are the different kinds of Yoga? Does the Bhagavad Gita say anything on this? From the previous chapter, we now understand the deep desires of the soul and its eternal connection with the supersoul. We understand how these fundamental hankerings of the soul are the very objectives that we try to achieve through the various avenues of this world; albeit unsuccessfully. Hence, we shall now discuss the proper processes which have been well documented in the ancient Vedic scriptures, that guide us to achieve this much elusive fulfillment missing in our lives- by satisfying the desires of the Soul. The process of uniting the soul and the Supersoul is also known as Yoga.

The [Bhagavad Gita](#) is considered to be one of the most sacred books in this world. It comprises seven hundred verses spoken by Sri Krishna, the Supreme Lord Himself, who had descended in this world about 5000 years ago, to give us a taste of His sweet eternal pastimes. The Bhagavad Gita encompasses the conversation between Sri Krishna and His friend Arjuna, in the middle of a battlefield, at a time when Arjuna was thoroughly disillusioned and confused as to what was his duty.

Sri Krishna, first of all, apprised Arjuna of the reality of our existence. All of us, including the various other life forms that exist, are spiritual beings, entrapped in a material body. The soul can neither be destroyed by any weapon, nor be damaged by water, fire or wind. The soul or the spirit, neither takes birth, nor does he ever

Website - www.thegaudiyatreasuresofbengal.com

suffer death. Instead, the soul goes through a process of transmigration, from one body to the next, in the quest of attaining perfection. The soul finally attains a stage of perfection when it is able to rekindle its lost relationship with the Supreme. Thus Lord Krishna taught Arjuna ,how the so-called happiness and grief, success and failure, relationships, hankering for name, fame and prosperity ,etc associated with this world, are actually based out of the assumption that we are our bodies. Forgetting our eternal identity, we try to build our identities based out of the temporary objects of this material world, and suffer in the process. Instead, we should align our engagements and relationships, in a way to suit our actual (eternal) objective - to perfect our existence. In other words we should stop acting on a bodily platform, and start acting on a spiritual platform. The process of Yoga helps us achieve this objective and enables us to harmonize our actions with our actual spiritual mission.

The Yoga ladder

Karma Yoga :

Sri Krishna explains that all the creatures of this world are born with certain inherent natures and thus act according to their tendencies. It is of no use trying to artificially renounce action, as the mind and the body of a conditioned person (entrapped soul) is completely dictated by the nature he was born with. Hence, one should perform the prescribed duties as per his nature, and dedicate the fruits of his work as an offering unto the Supreme Lord. The key here is not to become attached to the results but act without desiring any profit or any claims of proprietorship.Thus though, one might not be able to change his activities,one can possibly change the consciousness with which he performs them. In this mood, without becoming envious or lusty, one should perform his prescribed actions, keeping the Lord in the center. Such a person is never bound up by the reactions of his work.This in a nutshell is the path of **karma Yoga**.

From the above descriptions, it is quite evident that the science of Yoga is not sectarian, or is not something that is restricted to a particular community or a religious belief. Instead, it is something that applies to all creatures who want a way out of their material entanglement.

Jnana Yoga:

Sri Krishna then continues that better than the process of Karma Yoga (non-fruitive action) described above, is the process of performing actions equipped with transcendental knowledge of the Supreme (**Jnana Yoga**).In order to help Arjuna get a taste of this higher knowledge, Krishna then explains to him, His own Supreme Position - how both He and Arjuna have taken several births before, but the difference between them is that though He remembers all of His previous births and activities, Arjuna does not. Sri Krishna reveals to Arjuna, that He Himself descends millennium after millennium ,whenever and wherever there is a decline in the religious practices, in order to annihilate the miscreants and deliver the pious, and to subsequently re-establish the religious principles. Sri Krishna further informs Arjuna how the different modes of material nature (modes of goodness,passion and ignorance) and the different types of work associated with these particular natures (

administrators, businessmen, laborers), have been actually created by Him, to suit the different desires of the various living entities. But though He is the creator of this system, yet He remains completely unaffected and unentangled by these modes of nature. Arjuna then learns how the great men of the past have perfected their lives, by performing their actions arming themselves with the sword of this transcendental knowledge about the Supreme Lord (Lord Krishna). Such a knowledgeable worker, whose every endeavour is devoid of sense gratification, is never bound up by the reactions of his work. Such a person, equipped with the weapon of Jnana (transcendental knowledge), is always satisfied and independent, although engaged in all kinds of undertakings.

After hearing Lord Krishna's instructions on both Karma (performing action) and the importance of Jnana (Transcendental knowledge), Arjuna got perplexed. He became confused as he found the path of action and cultivating knowledge to be contradictory to each other. Arjuna therefore inquired, whether renunciation of work or work in devotion - which of the two was superior. Lord Krishna then explained to him that work in devotion is always superior to renouncing work. He further explained that one who neither hates nor desires the fruits of his activities is actually renounced. Such a person easily overcomes the modes of material nature and is completely liberated. The steadily devoted souls attain unadulterated peace because they offer the results of their activities unto the Supreme Lord, whereas one who is not in union with the divine (not following the Yogic processes) is greedy for the fruits of his labor and gets entangled in the process. Therefore Lord Krishna instructed Arjuna, to perform his duty and steadily act for the satisfaction of Krishna. At the same time, Arjuna was instructed to fix up his consciousness upon the Supreme Lord and act with the knowledge that Sri Krishna is the supreme mystic, the master of all creation and the true goal of all sacrifices & austerities. By performing actions in such a mood, one attains true peace and fulfillment, which is otherwise unattainable by an embodied being.

Dhyana Yoga:

Lord Krishna then went even one step further and explained to Arjuna the very essence of Yoga - to focus one's mind and consciousness unto His lotus feet. He explained that a person who is elevated in Yoga, neither acts for sense gratification nor engages himself in fruitive activities (instead he dedicates the fruits of his work unto the Supreme). He explained that one who is regulated in his habits of eating, sleeping, recreation and work is qualified to practice yoga and can mitigate all material pains in the process (*Yuktahara viharasya yukta cestasya karmasu, Yukta svanavabodhasya yogo bhavati dukha ha*)

By constantly controlling one's mind, withdrawing it from the objects of sense enjoyment, and proceeding with utmost determination and faith, one must fix his consciousness upon the Supreme Lord, and thereby ultimately attain the highest perfection of transcendental happiness.

As a lamp doesn't waver in a windless place, similarly, a yogi always remains steady meditating upon the Supreme.

And what is the consciousness of such a yogi ?

A true yogi observes the Supreme Lord in all beings and also sees every being belonging to the Supreme. He sees the same Supreme Lord everywhere.*(Sarva bhutastham atmaanam Sarva bhutani catmaani, iksate yoga yuktatma sarvatra sama darshanah).*

As a matter of fact, all living entities (jiva) are the servants of the Supreme Lord and no matter what material condition he is entrapped in, the fact remains that his identity is ultimately spiritual and he is a part and parcel of the same lord. A yogi, whose consciousness is situated on a transcendental platform, is able to perceive these things as they are and can act being equipped with such realizations.

The process of 'Dhyana Yoga' explained above by Sri Krishna, however, seemed impractical and unendurable to Arjuna, who then exclaimed that the mind is very restless, unsteady and turbulent. Arjuna, one of the greatest fighters to have ever graced this world, then remarked that it was easier for him to control the mighty wind than to control his own mind.

cancalam hi manah Krishna
pramathi balavad dridham

Website - www.thegaudiyatreasuresofbengal.com

> *tasyaham nigraham manye*
> *vayor iva su duskaram*
> *(Bhagavad Gita - 6.34)*

To this Sri Krishna replied, that the task of controlling one's mind was indeed very difficult indeed, but it could be achieved by suitable practice and detachment.

Arjuna then enquired about the fate of an unsuccessful yogi, to which Sri Krishna replied that - The unsuccessful yogi, after many many years of enjoyment in the higher planets, takes birth in a family of righteous people or into a family of rich aristocracy. Or else he takes birth in a family of yogis, who are great in wisdom, and receiving their association, he revives the divine consciousness from his previous life and automatically becomes attracted to the yogic principles. Such an inquisitive transcendentalist, striving for yoga, stands always above the ritualistic principles of the scriptures. A yogi, after many many births of practice, being washed of all contamination, ultimately attains the supreme goal. Hence Lord Krishna here declares that there is never a loss for one who walks the spiritual path endeavouring to attain the Supreme truth. Even if he does not achieve the ultimate goal in his current lifetime, he continues exactly from where he left off, in his subsequent birth.

But who is the greatest of all the Yogis? What are the activities of one who is the most intimately united with the Supreme Lord in Yoga?

Bhakti Yoga:

Sri Krishna explains in above verses, that by executing the processes of strictly controlling one's mind and senses (dhyana), one should try to reach the transcendental platform, which is free from all the dualities of this material world. Situated in such transcendence, one should try to meditate upon the Supreme Lord with an unwavering mind. Such an elevated yogi is always conscious of the Supreme Lord and sees everything in relation to Him.

But the highest of all the yogis is one, who with great faith always abides by the Supreme Lord and constantly thinks of Him within Himself, rendering transcendental loving service unto Him.Sri Krishna proclaims, that such a yogi (devotee) ,is the most intimately united with Him in yoga and the highest of all.

> *Yoginaam api sarvesam mad gatenantar atmana*
>
> *Sradhavan bhajate yo mam ,sa me yuktatamo matah*
>
> *(BG 6.47)*

The process of Karma Yoga slowly leads one to enter the domain of transcendental knowledge. Performing work equipped with higher knowledge, gradually situates one in transcendence, liberating him from the bondages of material nature. Controlling his mind & senses, and by suitable practice and detachment, such a transcendentalist is able to successfully meditate upon the Supreme Lord ,who is the cause of all and everything that is, and thereby he further advances in his spiritual life. But the culmination of all the yogic processes of Karma, Jnana and Dhyana is to ultimately reestablish the loving relationship with the Supreme Lord and render loving devotional service unto Him, as confirmed by the Lord in Bhagavad Gita. Such a Yogi, who serves the Supreme with Bhakti (unalloyed

Love), is the most intimately united with Him in yoga, and is the highest of all the yogis. The devotees (bhaktas) of the Lord are hence residing on the highest platform of yoga, and are unleashing themselves to realize the ultimate treasures of love of God - and are enroute to achieving the complete perfection of their lives.

What is Sanatan Dharma?

Dharma is often interpreted as "duty," "religion" or "religious duty" and yet its definition is more profound, defying the concise English translation. The word 'Dharma' originates from the Sanskrit root "*dhri*," which means "to sustain." Another correlated meaning of 'Dharma' is 'that which is indispensable and fundamental to something'. The word 'Sanatan' translates to 'eternal' and the phrase 'Sanatan Dharma' alludes to that which is eternally integral to a living entity. That which is

'Sanatan' does not have either a beginning or an end. Likewise, 'Sanatan Dharma' is timeless, non-sectarian and not limited by any boundaries. Religion conveys the idea of faith, and faith of a person may change. But 'Sanatan Dharma' is that which cannot be changed. For instance liquidity cannot be taken away from water, nor can heat be taken away from fire.

Eternal Nature (Sanatan Dharma) vs Temporary Nature (Naimittika Dharma)

The eternal characteristics or nature (svabhava) of an entity (Vastu) is its Sanatan Dharma. When an entity comes into existence, it is created along with an original fundamental nature. Later, due to circumstances, when this entity comes in contact with other entities, it might develop a change in its nature. Over time, this changed or acquired nature (naimittika dharma) becomes firmly established and accompanies the entity just like its original eternal nature (Sanatan Dharma). But this acquired nature should not be mistaken as the original nature of the entity. These changed characteristics of the concerned entity (vastu) are called 'nisarga'.

For example, water is an entity, and liquidity is its eternal nature (Sanatan Dharma). But when this same water is frozen into solid ice, then its liquidity is no more apparent. Instead, the solidity of ice becomes its acquired characteristics (naimittika dharma). But the 'nisarga' or acquired nature of an entity is never permanent. It arises due to a temporary circumstance and when the circumstance changes, the entity regains its original nature.

The original nature or the Sanatan Dharma of an entity is eternal. Even when a modified nature (naimittika dharma) is manifested, the original nature prevails, although it may be dormant. In the course of time when the conditions are favorable, the original nature manifests itself openly once more. In our example, the solid ice changes into liquid water as soon as the freezing conditions are eliminated.

What is the 'Sanatan Dharma' of Man ?

According to S*anatan Dharma*, the eternal and intrinsic nature of a living entity (*atman*), including Man, is to perform *seva* (service). *Sanatan dharma*, being transcendental, refers to the universal and axiomatic laws that are beyond our shifting belief systems. If we deeply study the world around us, we would not find anyone who is not serving someone else. The father serves the son, the son serves his father, the wife serves his husband, the doctor serves his patients, the king serves his subjects, and so on. If someone has no one to serve, then he/she keeps a pet in his/her house and serves him. Thus, all of us are bound to serve, because by nature, the soul is a servant, and service is a

Website - www.thegaudiyatreasuresofbengal.com

natural characteristic (Sanatan Dharma) of the soul.

The Vedic literatures, which are the oldest scriptures in the world, give us some much-needed insight on this subject. The Vedic scriptures, composed mainly in Sanskrit, and which encompasses a huge volume of texts and manuscripts, provide a detailed analysis and a first-hand experience of significant historical events, with a purpose to teach us the science of life. The Vedic scriptures, that form the very basis of the tenets of Sanatan Dharma, conclude that Man achieves the perfection of his existence only when he dovetails his eternal nature in serving the Supreme Lord. Instead, if he chooses to serve his own senses or his false ego, then he encircles himself in a material quagmire that only makes him suffer in multiple ways.

Jivera svarupa haya Krishera Nityadasa

Krishnera tathastha shakti bhedabeda prakasha

(Chaitanya Charitamrita)

Website - www.thegaudiyatreasuresofbengal.com

The original nature of a living entity is to be an eternal servant of Lord Krishna. The living entity is the marginal potency of the Supreme Lord Krishna and is simultaneously one and different from the Lord.

The service attitude that a soul possesses towards Supersoul, is not based on any obligation, but is instead built on a foundation of a loving relationship. The whole purpose of our existence is to render loving devotional service unto the Supreme Lord, recognizing Him to be our ever well-wisher and our eternal object of love. Out of 8.4 million species of life, a human being is the most conscious and is perfectly equipped to attain complete spiritual realization. Hence one should not waste the precious human form of life and instead utilize it for God-realization from an early age. If we examine the life and history of people living in various parts of the world, we shall come to realize that faith in God is universal and a natural characteristic of people in general. Even the uncivilized tribes living in the forest, worship trees, rivers, mountains, etc, and exhibit their reverence towards the divine.

Living entities, including man, are spirit souls that are part and parcel of the Supreme Lord. The soul can neither be destroyed by any weapon, nor be damaged by water, fire or wind. The soul or the spirit, neither takes birth, nor does he ever suffer death. Instead, the soul goes through a process of transmigration, from one body to the next, in a quest of attaining perfection. The soul finally attains a stage of perfection when it is able to rekindle its lost relationship with the Supreme.

Contrary to popular beliefs, Yoga is not merely a set of physical exercises. Instead it is a gradual process of uniting the soul with the Supersoul, thereby perfecting the existence of a living being. Sri Krishna states in Bhagavad Gita that the highest of all the yogis is one, who with great faith always abides by the Supreme Lord and constantly thinks of Him within Himself, rendering transcendental loving service unto Him. Sri Krishna proclaims, that such a yogi (devotee), is the most intimately united with Him in yoga and the highest of all.

Yoginaam api sarvesam mad gatenantar atmana

Sradhavan bhajate yo mam, sa me yuktatamo matah

(BG 6.47)

Sri Krishna thus confirms in Bhagavad Gita that rendering transcendental loving service unto Him, is the highest truth and the ultimate path to achieving perfection in one's life.

The science of Life :

Spirit and matter are fundamentally opposed to each other. One can either live in spiritual or else in material consciousness. Likewise, material and spiritual attachments are inversely proportional to each other. Lord Krishna, the Supreme Lord, is the master of countless potencies.

parasya saktir vividhaiva sruyate - His energies are innumerable and immeasurable (Svetasvatara Upanishad 6.8)

These potencies can be grouped primarily into internal, marginal, and external. The internal energy of the Supreme Lord constitutes the eternal, blissful, and cognizant spiritual world. Those who possess a spiritual consciousness and seek the shelter of the Supreme Lord fall within the purview of the Lord's internal energy (Hladini shakti). On the other hand, this temporary world of matter falls within the purview of the Lord's external energy (Bahiranga shakti). The living entities of this world, however, belong to a third category. They belong to the marginal potency or the 'tatastha shakti' of the Supreme Lord. 'Tata' refers to the region between land and water, and hence it holds the properties of both. Therefore 'tata' cannot be referred to as belonging purely to either land or water. Similarly, the living entities of this world have a choice to serve either the world of spirit or the world of matter. Though the living entity is a part and parcel of the Supreme Lord and spiritual by nature, yet sometimes it may become overwhelmed by this temporary world of dull matter. Those living beings who grow bewildered by the illusory energy (Maya) of the Lord and consequently try to enjoy this temporary material world, become controlled by the external potency (bahiranga shakti) of the Supreme Lord. These unfortunate souls deviate from their constitutional position as a servant of the Supreme Lord and indulge in sense gratification by serving their material senses and trying to Lord over matter. However, their efforts only die in frustration as flickering sensual pleasures can never fully satisfy a living being who is eternally hankering for pure spiritual bliss. Such a misguided person, then attempts to rediscover the loving relationship it once possessed with the Supreme Lord, within the purview of matter, and thus gets entangled with material possessions. But in the process, neither does he get satisfied, nor the person/s he is serving becomes fully satisfied- due to the misdirected nature of such service, which should be directed towards the Supreme Lord instead. On the other hand, those wise living entities, who choose to engage in the devotional service of the Supreme Lord, become controlled by the Lord's internal energy (Hladini shakti) and are protected by Him.

Misdirected service - Root cause of all evil

A spirit soul is always in love. Constitutionally, it is meant to love and be loved. This propensity of the soul to render loving devotional service is completely satisfied when it is directed towards God, the Supreme Spirit. Katha Upanishad

Website - www.thegaudiyatreasuresofbengal.com

states that the Supreme Lord is the Supreme eternal amongst all the other eternal beings. He is the fundamental conscious being among all the other conscious beings *(Nityo nityanam cetanas cetananam)*. A spirit soul is a part and parcel of the Supreme Lord and is bound to Him by love.

However, when a living entity or a spirit soul, grows forgetful of this eternal loving relationship with the supreme, he gets overwhelmed with this temporary world of matter. As the soul always seeks love (devotional service), therefore when it loses touch with the divine, it becomes attached to inferior material objects. However, a loving relationship with the Supreme Lord that bestows ecstatic spiritual bliss can never be substituted by love and attachment for dull matter, which only renders flickering sensual pleasures. As self-satisfaction grows far-fetched, one begins indulging in serving his senses more and more. The greater the extent of one's material entanglement, the further is one's alienation from his eternal spiritual reality. The absence of divine love frustrates the soul because the soul only hankers for eternal spiritual bliss.

Just like the Supreme Lord, a living entity is also eternal (sat), cognizant (cid), and full of bliss (ananda). The Supreme Lord is like the sun while the living entities are like sunlight. Living entities are like sparks emanating from the blazing fire of the Supreme Lord. So though the living entities are qualitatively the same with the Lord, the difference lies in their quantity. When this living entity disregards God and forgets Him, he at once comes under the influence of material nature. At that time, he develops several temporary characteristics (Naimittika Dharma) that eclipse his eternal inclination to serve the Supreme Lord. Consequently, this temporary nature of the living being overshadows his eternal blissful nature, and may even manifest itself in the form of greed, anger, lust, envy, depression, anxiety, etc. However, it must be remembered that the original eternal nature (Sanatan Dharma) of the living entity is never lost. It unveils itself at the appropriate time, as soon as the living being rejects his degraded material consciousness. Just as vapour transforms itself back into its

Website - www.thegaudiyatreasuresofbengal.com

original form of water, as soon as the boiling conditions are eliminated, similarly the living entity regains his original blissful nature as soon as he awakens his eternal loving relationship with the Supreme Lord.

Is Sanatan Dharma Sectarian?

The sun may be called by different names but remains one no matter how widely we travel. Similarly, God is one though He might be called upon differently by different people. Likewise, the laws of physics or mathematics are universal, although students might study them in various universities. Similarly, though one might accept a particular authorized religious tradition, the ultimate goal to render devotional service unto the Supreme prevails. Those belonging to some sectarian faith will wrongly consider that Sanatan dharma is also sectarian, but if we go deeper into the matter and consider it in the light of modern science, we shall discover that Sanatan dharma is the affair of all the people of the world, nay, of all the living entities of the universe. Hence, most adherents prefer to call their tradition 'Sanatan dharma' rather than using the more recent term, "Hinduism", which they consider has sectarian connotations.

Does Sanatan Dharma imply rejection of matter?

Website - www.thegaudiyatreasuresofbengal.com

Now one may ask whether practicing the teachings of Sanatan Dharma imply the rejection of anything that is material. One may also wonder if he/she ought to give up their dwelling in the city, let go of their phones/gadgets, and take up a residence in the forests or the mountains instead. Well, the precise answer is 'No'. When we say that one needs to give up matter, what we propose is that one abandons his/her illusory perception of 'I' and 'Mine' that originates from a material identification of the self. In other words, one needs to renounce serving his/her material senses and instead try and use everything in the service of the Supreme Lord, which is in his/her ultimate spiritual interest.

Website - www.thegaudiyatreasuresofbengal.com

When one practices 'Sanatan Dharma' and acts to accomplish their spiritual objectives, then one can utilize matter to achieve those ends. For example, one can use the internet to read this website article. One can buy spiritual books online, to enhance his/her spiritual understanding. One can even write books/articles, compose songs/music, etc in order to help others in their spiritual journey. When matter is utilized for spiritual goals, then it no longer remains a part of the material energy. As long as one lives in this material world, and possesses a material body, he/she requires to interact with matter. But if the purpose of that interaction is simply to serve one's own senses, then the particular person acts on a material platform. Instead, if one interacts with matter in order to serve and please the Supreme Lord, then one no longer entangles himself in this material predicament. So though a spiritualist interacts with matter, just like a materialist, yet there prevails a stark difference when it comes to their consciousness. A materialist puts himself at the center of his world while a spiritualist places the Supreme Lord at the center of all his actions.

Website - www.thegaudiyatreasuresofbengal.com

*atmendriya priti vancha taare bali
'kama'
krishnendriya-priti-iccha dhare
'prema' nama*

(Chaitanya Charitamrita)

-

The desire to gratify one's own senses is called kama (lust), but the desire to please the senses of Lord Krishna is known as prema (love).

One who recognizes Sanatan Dharma, will always endeavor to revive his/her eternal relationship with Krishna, the Supreme Lord. He shall no longer identify with matter and possess no interest in petty sense gratification. Instead, matter then becomes a means to engage in loving devotional service of the Supreme. Such a man's involvement with this world is no longer based upon a false conception of the self and is no more motivated by sensual pleasures. He no longer traps himself in an illusory web of 'I' and 'Mine'. Engaging in selfless loving devotional service unto the Supreme, he successfully revives his eternal, blissful, and cognizant nature.

Practicing Sanatan Dharma :

The Bhagavad Gita teaches how this material world is exceedingly difficult for a living entity to overcome *(mama maya duratyaya)*. But this incredibly challenging objective is easily accomplished by those who surrender unto Sri Krishna, the Supreme Lord and seek His divine shelter *(mam eva ye prapadyante mayam etam taranti te)*. Such a person can control his mind, transcend material nature, and even his material desires. Such a perfect devotee rejoices in boundless spiritual bliss and is not shaken even amidst the greatest of difficulties. This certainly is actual independence - freedom from all miseries (anxiety, depression, fear, etc) arising out of material contact. Such a person identifies everything as part and parcel of the Supreme and tries to engage them in the service of the Supreme Lord. Everything else takes a backseat, while serving the Supreme becomes his primary objective.

Website - www.thegaudiyatreasuresofbengal.com

Now, one might question as to how one can take shelter or serve the Supreme Lord practically and revive this state of spiritual consciousness. Does it only demand an adjustment of intellectual perception or does it also require certain spiritual practices? The ancient Vedic scriptures proclaim that chanting the holy Name of Supreme Lord Hari is the only practical and effective means of cultivating spiritual realization (devotion) in this present day and age. Nothing else is as powerful.

Harer nama harer nama harer namaiva kevalam

kalau nasty-eva nasty-eva nasty-eva gatir anyathaa

(Brhad Naradiya Purana)

Website - www.thegaudiyatreasuresofbengal.com

In this age of Kali the only means of deliverance is chanting of the holy name of Lord Hari. There is no other way. There is no other way. There is no other way.

Love for the Supreme Lord is not something that can be achieved artificially from an external source. It is eternally existing within the hearts of all living entities. When the heart is purified by the process of regular hearing and chanting the holy names, glories of the Supreme Lord, this eternal love awakens and reveals itself once more.

*nitya-siddha Krishna-prema
'sadhya' kabhu naya,*

*sravanadi suddha chitte karaye
udaya*

(Chaitanya Charitamrta, Madhya, 22.107)

Website - www.thegaudiyatreasuresofbengal.com

Pure love for Krishna is eternally established in the hearts of the living entities. It is not something to be gained from an external source. When one's heart is purified by the regular hearing and chanting of Krishna's holy name and glories, this love naturally awakens.

How old is the Indian civilization and its Sanatan Dharma?

In his Discourse on Sanskrit and Its Literature, given at the College of France, Professor Bournouf addresses this question as to how old is the Indian civilization and its Sanatan Dharma? He says, "We will study India with its philosophy and its myths, its literature, its laws and its language. Nay it is more than India, it is a page of the origin of the world that we will attempt to decipher."

Website - www.thegaudiyatreasuresofbengal.com

Max Mueller observed in history of Sanskrit Literature, "In the Rig-veda we shall have before us more real antiquity than in all the inscriptions of Egypt or Ninevah...the Veda is the oldest book in existence.."

The famous German thinker, Schopenhaur, remarked in the introduction to his book, 'The Upanishads', "In the whole world there is no study so beneficial and so elevating as that of the Upanishads. It has been the solace of my life (and) it will be the solace of my death."

What are the Vedas ?

Before investigating the antiquity of the Indian or its Vedic civilization, we should first of all try and learn more about the Vedic literatures. The Sanskrit root vid means 'to know'. Hence the word 'Veda' means knowledge. The term Vedic refers to the literature and teachings contained in the Vedas. The Vedic scriptures are the spiritual literature of ancient Indian culture, written primarily in the Sanskrit language. They comprise a huge collection of books encompassing a wide variety of subjects, including but not restricted to material

Website - www.thegaudiyatreasuresofbengal.com

(mundane), religious (ritualistic) and spiritual (monotheistic) knowledge.

The Vedas are immense both in their size and scope. Its sheer volume easily surpasses any other religious scriptures of this world. Vedas even surpass the lengthy ancient works such as Homer's epics and the sacred cannon of China. For instance, Mahabharata, one of the Vedic epics, has 110,000 four-line stanzas, making it the world's largest poem – approximately eight times as lengthy as Iliad and Odyssey combined. Ramayana, another Vedic epic, consists of 24,000 couplets. The Vedic literature comprises not only of the Rig, Yajur, Atharva and the Sama vedas but also of Upanishads, Puranas, Bhagavad Gita and itihasas like Ramayana & Mahabharata. It encompasses all literatures that uphold the Vedic teachings, tradition and culture.

The Vedic literature not only deals with life as we understand it but it also deals with the knowledge of nature, universe, and a grand hierarchy of living beings – nonhumans, humans & humanoids. There is a large section of the Vedas that deal with detailed accounts of the non-material worlds beyond the fabric of time and space. For the earthly humans, however, the Vedas prescribe a balance between their spiritual and material lives. The Vedic social system combines the material impetus with the spiritual dynamics and places a great emphasis on civilization as a precise tool for both material and spiritual upliftment.

Website - www.thegaudiyatreasuresofbengal.com

So how old is the Indian Civilization? - Digging into the Past

#1 A city Dating back to 7500 BC

As was announced on January 16, 2002, that the Indian scientists found pieces of wood, remains of pots, fossil bones, etc near the coast of Surat, Indian Science and Technology Minister Murli Manohar Joshi told a news conference. He said, "Some of these artifacts recovered by the National Institute of Ocean Technology from the site, such as the log of wood date back to 7500 bce, which is indicative of a very ancient culture in the present Gulf of Cambay, that got submerged subsequently." Current belief is that the first cities appeared around 3500 bce in the valley of Sumer, where Iraq now stands. "We can safely say from the antiquities and the acoustic images of the geometric structures that there was human activity in the region more than 9,500 years ago (7500 BC)," said S.N. Rajguru, an independent archaeologist.

Website - www.thegaudiyatreasuresofbengal.com

#2 Discovering River Saraswati

The legend of the mighty Saraswati river has lived on in India since time immemorial. The ancient Vedic scriptures are full of tantalizing hymns about it being the life-stream of the people. References to river Saraswati can be widely found in the Rig Veda, Mahabharata, Ramayana, Bhagavata Purana, Vamana Purana, Upanishads, etc. The Vedic scriptures are the oldest in the world and are atleast 5000 years old.

An Indian and French archaeological field team on the ground, coordinating with a French SPOT satellite in space, have discovered that the Saraswati River, as described in the Vedas,

Website - www.thegaudiyatreasuresofbengal.com

is a fact, not mythology. Vividly exposing the signatures of old rivers and their branches, data from SPOT shows that the river Saraswati did exist. The Satellite's sensors and pointable optics reveal the dried bed of a river stretching from the present Ghaggar River and flowing four miles wide, in the region of India, west of what is now Delhi. In what is now Punjab, the Satellite imagery has shown the Saraswati's bed to be twelve miles wide. From space, researchers can detect that Saraswati had several tributaries, watering an immense area of fertile soil. Traces of artificial canals watering remote agricultural locations are also visible.

#3 Ancient Hindu Temples found worldwide

The Archaeological survey of India unearthed a monolithic sandstone Shiva Linga of 9th century CE during its conservation project at Vietnam's Cham temple complex in My Son sanctuary. India's External Affairs Minister Dr S Jaishankar who shared the news on Twitter (on May 27,2020) termed it as 'Reaffirming a civilizational connect'.

The Chinese city of Quanzhou bears ample proof of the cultural connection between ancient India and China. The famous Kaiyuan temple – a major tourist destination – in Quanzhou has carvings that were influenced by Hindu styles. Hundreds of sculptures and carvings were excavated in the city and surrounding areas in the middle of the last century. They threw up the proof that tamil sea traders had made Quanzhou an important port-of-call, approximately a thousand years ago. The Quanzhou maritime museum presently houses these exhibits and among them are Vishnu and Lakshmi idols.

A Cangkuang villager hunting for termites under a tree discovered a sharp hand-carved stone. Further investigation revealed that the

Website - www.thegaudiyatreasuresofbengal.com

location was the site of an ancient Vedic/Hindu temple. Ony Djubiantono, head of **West Java's** Bandung Archeology Agency says, "Based on a preliminary finding of various remains there are indications that this is a Hindu temple built in the seventh or eighth century."

The ancient Nandeeshwara(Shiva) temple at **Malleswaram** was discovered recently but it has stood for 7,000 years on that spot. Being buried over the years hasn't diminished its aura at all. The temple was discovered only recently when the land was being dug up and it was found that the temple had remained untouched over the years. At the far end of the temple courtyard, stood the deity of Nandi with eyes painted in Gold and from his mouth a stream of water flowed directly onto a Shiva Linga made out of the same black stone at a lower level.

Nearly 40 kilometers from the **Thai-Cambodia border** the Chen Sran temple has been discovered in the jungle of the northern Preah Vihear province. It was built in the ninth or tenth century, and is dedicated to the Vedic tradition. The temple stands 15 meters tall, and is 150 meters in length by 100 meters wide.

Website - www.thegaudiyatreasuresofbengal.com

Nearly 50 percent of the structure is damaged and most of its artifacts have been plundered, even though there is no decent road to the temple.

Archaeologists have found a statue of Nandi, the sacred bull that carried the Hindu god Shiva, among the ruins of what is believed to be an ancient temple at an excavation site in **Yogyakarta** in Indonesia.

Oldest ever Idol discovered so far is the Lion-Man ivory sculpture, which is estimated to be 40,000 years old. It was discovered in the Hohlenstein-Stadel, a German cave in 1939. This 29.6 cm (11.7 inches) in height, 5.6 cm wide, and 5.9 cm thick sculpture was carved out of woolly mammoth ivory using a flint stone knife. The Vedic scriptures teach us that Krishna had appeared in this divine form of a half-man, half-lion with a lion face, in order to protect His devotee Prahlada and to stop the spread of irreligion, personified by the demon Hiranyakasipu. The Supreme Lord in this form is worshipped as Lord Narasimha.

Website - www.thegaudiyatreasuresofbengal.com

An ancient Vishnu idol has been found during excavation in an old village in Russia's Volga region, raising questions about the prevalent view on the origin of ancient Russia. The idol found in Staraya (old) Maina village dates back to 7-10th century AD. Staraya Maina village in Ulyanovsk region was a highly populated city about 1700 years ago (much older than Kiev) and so fat it is believed to be the mother of all Russian cities. "We may consider it incredible, but we have ground to assert that Middle-Volga region was the original land of Ancient Rus. This is a hypothesis, but a hypothesis, which requires thorough research," Reader of Ulyanovsk State University's archaeology

Website - www.thegaudiyatreasuresofbengal.com

department Dr Alexander Kozhevin told state-run television Vesti.

#4 Major Anthropology Find Reported in India

Scientists have found evidence of the oldest human habitation in India, dating to 2 million years, on the banks of the Subarnarekha River. The 30-mile stretch between Ghatshila in the province of Jharkhand and Mayurbhanj in Orissa has reportedly yielded tools that suggest the site could be unique in the world, with evidence of human habitation without a break from 2 million years ago to 5,000 B.C. which makes it more important than even the Aldovai Gorge in East Africa, the Somme Valley of France, Stonehenge in England, the Narmada basin in Madhya Pradesh and the Velamadurai-Pallavaram rectangle in Tamil Nadu. Anthropologist S. Chakraborty told the Calcutta Telegraph: *"There are no signs of terra incognito (a break in the continuum) in the Subarnarekha valley, unlike any other site in India. Some of the heavier tools resemble those found in the East African stone-age shelters, used by the Australopithecus."*

Website - www.thegaudiyatreasuresofbengal.com

On the banks of Suvarnarekha, Gopiballavpur

#5 Tamil Brahmi Script Found in Egypt

A few years ago, a broken storage jar with inscriptions in Tamil Brahmi script has been excavated at Quseir-al-Qadim, an ancient port with a Roman settlement on the Red Sea coast of Egypt. This Tamil Brahmi script has been dated to the first century B.C. The same inscription is incised twice on the opposite sides of the jar. The inscribed text is "paanai oRi" which means 'pot suspended in a rope net'. This fragmentary vessel was identified as a storage jar made in India.

Website - www.thegaudiyatreasuresofbengal.com

Vedic Culture and today's world

The above evidence clearly hints at the existence of a worldwide flourishing Vedic civilization, not so long ago, signifying the importance and authenticity of the Vedic scriptures. It shows that our forefathers walked the Vedic path to attain the higher essential spiritual goals of life. As a matter of fact, the Vedic civilization, being the oldest, has influenced every major culture and religion around the world that we know today, and can be declared as the parent of humanity. The philosopher and researcher Edward Pococke also wrote about this conclusion in his book India in Greece. He states: "Sir William Jones concluded that the Hindus had an immemorial antiquity with the old Persians, Ethiopians and Egyptians, the Phoenicians, Greeks and Tuscans, the Scythians or Goths, and the Celts, the Chinese, Japanese and Peruvians."

Pococke continues in his observation: "Now the whole of the society of Greece, civil and military, must strike one as being eminently Asiatic, much of it specially Indian. I shall

Website - www.thegaudiyatreasuresofbengal.com

demonstrate that these evidences were but the attendant tokens of Indian colonization with its corresponding religion and language. I shall exhibit dynasties disappearing from India, western India, to appear again in Greece, clans who fought upon the plains of Troy." Therefore, since Greece is supposed to be the origins of European culture, and since Greece displays much of the same culture as India, we can say that the pre-Christian culture of Europe was Vedic".

William Durant, author of the 10-volume Story of Civilization, wrote, "India was the motherland of our race, and Sanskrit the mother of European languages. She was the mother of our philosophy, of our mathematics, of the ideals embodied in Christianity, of self-government and democracy. Mother India is in many ways the mother of us all." The above references indicate that the Vedic culture was a global faith, a world influence. This is given further credence in the remarks of Ctesias, the Greek writer, who states "The Hindus were as numerous as all the other nations put together."

The Ultimate Message of the Vedas

The Vedas are compared to a desire tree because they contain all things knowable by man. They deal with mundane necessities as well as spiritual realization. The Vedas contain regulated principles of knowledge covering social, political, religious, economic, military, medicinal, chemical, physical, metaphysical subject matter and above all specific directions for spiritual realization. The essential teachings of Vedic literatures can be broadly categorized into three headings:

Sambandha: Understanding the answers to the questions, "Who am I? Who is God? What is my relation with God? Why am I suffering in this world?"

Abhideya: The process of reviving our lost relationship with the Supreme Lord.

Prayojana: Attaining the ultimate fruit of Love of God.

The Indian Varna System

The Indian Varna system (caste system), which is often painted negatively and presented likewise even in school textbooks, is perhaps one of the most misinterpreted social hierarchies of the world. It is popularly accepted that the Indian caste system is at least 3000 years old, though an analysis of the Vedic literatures suggests that it is perhaps as old as Sanatan Dharma (Hinduism) itself. This article attempts to exhibit the system of Varna (class) and Ashrama (order) as it had been originally conceived and how it has gradually degenerated with time. The article also seeks to establish

Website - www.thegaudiyatreasuresofbengal.com

how the caste system is an integral part of any successful society and an indispensable tool to ensure its survival.

The essence of the Indian Varna system :

It is imperative to determine the 'adhikara' or the qualification of a person before he undertakes any action. This 'adhikara' can be classified into two – 'qualification for a certain action' and 'the extent of such qualification'. Although a person can act, he might not be able to execute the action suitably to produce the desired results. Therefore, if the qualification of a person is not taken into consideration, it cannot be concluded decisively whether his actions will yield the expected results. Therefore, it is essential to accept a Guru or a spiritual master, someone who is experienced and capable of performing this much-required evaluation. It has to be recognized that accepting a Guru or a spiritual master is not a matter of formality or mere fashion, as is the case in modern times. Instead, one should perform a painstaking search to identify the most suitable person who can be his Guru. If such a Guru is not found in one's town, then one should continue his search elsewhere. One should be very diligent and thorough in accepting one's Guru. Holding the required qualifications is the fundamental requirement for any action. It is for the same reason that one's eligibility is thoroughly reviewed in a job interview before his recruitment. Similarly, in the course of life, it is exceedingly important to evaluate one's nature and inclinations (qualifications) to recognize his/her appropriate path.

Qualification or 'adhikara' can be inherent (intrinsic) or circumstantial. Life of an individual can be classified into three stages – the educational phase, the period of employment, and life after retirement. During the educational phase of life, a person studies books, associates with others, sees others working, and accepts others' teachings. That nature that arises prominently during this period of life forms the intrinsic characteristics of an individual. A person associates with his family and receives their instructions. But, it is entirely possible that such a person may develop a nature that is quite contrary to his family members. That nature which is manifest after education and before one enters his/her working life is the intrinsic nature of a person.

The Vedic scriptures that form the basis of Sanatan Dharma (Hinduism) broadly classify this intrinsic nature of an individual into four varnas (classes) - brahmana (priestly class), Kshatriya (warriors), Vaishya (mercantile class), and Shudra (those who are inclined to serve others). Those who are honest, inclined to cultivate knowledge, possess sense control, tolerance, purity, mercy, and who faithfully worship the Supreme Lord belong to the Brahmanical nature.

Those who possess courage, stamina, determination, agility, fearlessness in battle, a charitable inclination, the ability to protect others, and the ability to influence others are of a Kshatriya nature.

Those who are inclined to trading and agriculture have a Vaishya nature. And those who support themselves by serving others have a shudra nature.

However, those who do not distinguish between proper and improper actions, have no inclination for fairness, who are fond of quarrels, are selfish, greedy, and disregard the rules of marriage are regarded as 'antyaja' or outcasts.

The Indian Caste system or the Caste system professed by Sanatan Dharma (Hinduism) classifies the individuals into these four classes. According to the Vedic scriptures, the true standards of human life manifest only in these four castes (varnas) – brahmana, Kshatriya, Vaishya, and Shudra. A person manifests qualities as per his nature. This nature can be intrinsic or circumstantial, as has been discussed before. If one does not act according to his/her nature, one's actions might not yield productive results. As it is hard to change one's nature once it has matured, hence it is advised that one maintains his body and pursues his spiritual objectives in accordance with his nature.

Efficacy of the Indian Varna system (Caste system) :

The division of the society into castes ensures that an individual is ideally engaged as per his natural traits, all the work is effectively done, and it also benefits the society at large. Any

Website - www.thegaudiyatreasuresofbengal.com

society that is not properly organized into these divisions of brahmana, Kshatriya, Vaishya, and Shudra will eventually fall. The Indian civilization, although it is exceedingly old and has suffered from several foreign invasions, has survived with its original components and characteristics due to its prevalent caste system. On the contrary, the Roman and Greek civilizations were much more powerful than the modern European nations. However, not only have these civilizations collapsed in course of time, but these races have also become devoid of their former qualities. These people have become so transformed that they no longer take pride in their old glories. But this is not the case with India. The Varnasrama system or the division of the society into caste and order had remained strong in India and as a result, their ancient culture was preserved.

If we closely analyze the modern European or American societies, we would realize that their remarkable features are due to the implementation of the caste system in their societies. Those who are fond of trading prefer similar occupations. Those who have Kshatriya nature join the military. Those who are Shudra by nature prefer menial service. The European nations have incorporated some aspects of the caste system but have not established it systematically. The advancement of a civilization is directly proportional to the degree of systemization of the caste system.

Website - www.thegaudiyatreasuresofbengal.com

Degradation of the Indian Varna system :

The Varnasrama system (division of the society into class and order) in India has declined with time and this is one of the primary reasons for the troubles and degeneration of this country. India could have otherwise taken a leadership role in guiding modern human civilization. Previously, the people were divided into castes according to their individual nature and qualifications. The caste system would ensure that civilization runs smoothly. There are several instances in the Vedic scriptures that establish the fact that caste was previously determined by evaluating one's nature and not just his/her lineage. In the Kshatriya (princely) dynasty of Narisyanta, the great sage Jatukarna was born who started a famous brahmana lineage called Agnivesyayana. In the Aila Kshatriya dynasty, Jahnu the son of Hotraka, became a brahmana. From king Vitatha of Bharadvaja's dynasty came Nara and Garga, who were brahmanas and whose sons, in turn, were Kshatriyas. From King Bharmyasva's Kshatriya line were born Satananda of the

Moudgalya gotra and Kripacharya. There are innumerable such examples. The systematic implementation of the caste system was instrumental in expanding the glories of Bharata. Egypt, China, and other nations used to seek guidance from the people of India with great reverence.

In Chaitanya Sikshamrita, it has been asserted how the scientific and proper implementation of the caste system continued to be practiced in India for a long time, until Jamadagni and his son Parasurama claimed to be brahmanas, although both of them possessed a Kshatriya mentality. By following a caste as opposed to their own nature, they created animosity between the two classes (brahmana and Kshatriya). Subsequently, the practice of judging one's caste solely based upon one's birth became firmly established.

As birth and lineage became the only determining factor of one's caste, conflict and exploitation became rampant in society. Those with no Brahmanical qualities but brahmanas only in name, introduced scriptures harboring selfish interests in their heart, thus cheating the other classes. Likewise, Kshatriyas, crowned as kings and possessing no Kshatriya qualities, were subsequently defeated in battles. Those without Vaishya nature became merchants and this greatly weakened the mercantile community. Similarly, laborers without the Shudra mentality and without the skills to perform a required task turned into thieves and dacoits. Being devoid of scriptural guidance, the country suffered from foreign invasions. The present pathetic state of India, once the guru of the whole world, is not due to its old age but due to the corruption of its ideal caste system.

The fallacy of birth determining caste : Who is a brahmana?

As previously discussed, there are four castes according to the Vedas – Brahmana, Kshatriya, Vaishya, and Shudra. The brahmanas or the priestly class are considered to be the most esteemed, followed by the Kshatriyas, Vaishyas, and the Shudras. This is confirmed in both the srutis and the smritis. Now the question arises as to who is a brahmana? The living entity, the body, the caste, the knowledge, religiosity – of these which is the brahmana?

If one argues that the living entity is the brahmana, then it must be noted that as per the Vedic scriptures, the living entity is a spirit soul that transmigrates from one body to the other. Sometimes it occupies the body of a brahmana, sometimes that of a Kshatriya, sometimes shudra, or at times even the body of other animals. The soul is part and parcel of the Lord and its transmigration occurs depending on the Karma (pious or impious credits) accumulated by the individual. So the living entity can definitely not be the brahmana.

If it is argued that the body is the brahmana, then it needs to be understood that the bodies of all living entities, starting from the body of a so-called brahmana down to that of a 'chandala' or a barbarian, are made of the same five gross elements (earth, water, fire, ether, and wind).

Birth, Death, and diseases equally affect all bodies. Furthermore, there is no law that brahmanas are white, the Kshatriyas are red, the vaishyas are yellow, etc. So there cannot be any distinction of caste based upon one's body. Additionally, when the son of a brahmana lights the funeral pyre of his dead father, he does not sin killing a brahmana. Hence the body is definitely not the brahmana.

So is one's lineage the brahmana? This also cannot be true as several great sages have been born of other living entities. Rsysringa was born from a deer, Kaushika muni was born of Kusa grass, Jambuka was born of a jackal, Valmiki was born from an anthill, Srila Vyasadeva was borne by a fisherman's daughter, Gautama was born from the back of a rabbit, Vasistha muni was born from Urvasi and sage Agastya was born from a pitcher. Therefore, lineage is definitely not the brahmana.

Is knowledge then the 'brahmana'? No this is not the case either as there have been great personalities in the past who were Kshatriyas or belonging to other castes possessing vast knowledge on Absolute truth. Yudhisthira

Maharaja was very learned and so was grandsire Bhishma. Both of these great gentlemen were Kshatriyas. Similarly, religiosity is also not the determining factor as there are innumerable references of kings donating Gold in charity to others.

Who then is a brahmana? This question has been very nicely answered by Yudhisthira Maharaja and it is recorded in the Vana Parva of Mahabharata. The snake asked, 'O Maharaja Yudhisthira, who is a brahmana and what is the object of knowledge? You are very intelligent, therefore I will be enlightened by your answer'. Maharaja Yudhisthira replied, 'A person who possesses truthfulness, charity, forgiveness, sobriety, gentleness, austerity, and lack of hatred - Such a person is a brahmana'. The snake then enquired - 'But, even Shudras possess these qualities. Many of them possess truthfulness, charity, freedom from anger, nonviolence, non-enviousness, and lack of hatred'. Maharaja Yudhisthira then clarified, 'If such symptoms are found in a shudra then he should never be considered to be a Shudra, just as a brahmana is not a brahmana if he does not possess these qualities. O snake! only a person

Website - www.thegaudiyatreasuresofbengal.com

who is endowed with the characteristics of a brahmana can be called a brahmana, otherwise he is simply a Shudra'.

Elsewhere the Brahma Sutras reveal -

> *tad abhava nirdharane ca pravrtteh*
>
> -
>
> *Whether a person belongs to a varna other than that of his birth may be ascertained by considering his qualities.*

The Shanti parva of Mahabharata narrates a similar pastime in which Bharadwaja muni had a similar doubt and he clarified the same with Bhrigu Maharaja. He asked that since there were innumerable categories of animate and inanimate living entities – how can one possibly determine their castes?

Bhrigu Maharaja replied that there was not much difference between the various castes. When Lord Brahma initially created this universe, all the living entities were endowed with godly qualities and they were all brahmanas. Later on, as people became degraded, they attained the designations of different varnas (castes). He went on to explain that when the brahmanas commit violence, speak lies, become greedy, earn their livelihood by any and all activities, lose their purity by committing sinful activities, then they become degraded into shudras. Hence, it is the qualities, and not one's birth and lineage, that determines whether a person is a brahmana. One who realizes the self, is always satisfied, devoid of faults like lust and anger, possesses qualities like peacefulness, self control, and is devoid of envy, thirst for material enjoyment, illusion and is untouched by pride, false ego and so on – such a person is a brahmana.

Innumerable incidents illustrating this fact are known to those who are well aware of Indian history. For example, Gadhi was the son of Kusika and belonged to the Chandra (moon) dynasty. He was the king of Kanyakubja. His son, Visvamitra, advanced to become a brahmana, a great Brahma rishi, by the strength of his austerities. Even the great king Bali Maharaja, bore sons, some of who became brahmanas and some of who became Kshatriyas. His brahmana sons came to be known as Baleya brahmanas, whereas his

Kshatriya sons came to be known as Baleya Kshatriyas.

Towards the perfect society – Incorporating the Varna system :

The Brahmanas represent the Lord's mouth, the Kshatriyas His arms, the Vaisyas His abdomen (belly, waist, thighs), and the Shudras are born of His legs. This has been confirmed in the Srimad Bhagavatam. Thus the implementation of the caste system is an arrangement by the Lord.

>sri-camasa uvacha
>Mukha-bahuru-padebhyah
>purusasyasramaih saha
>catvaro jajnire varna
>gunair vipradayah prithak
>(Srimad Bhagavatam, 11.5.2)

However, on a spiritual plane, all living entities are part and parcels of the Supreme Lord. The purpose of the caste system is to engage individuals, as per their nature and qualities, in the service of the Lord. Such a system is auspicious for the individual and helps elevate his consciousness. It is also beneficial for society at large. A particular individual is qualified for engaging in actions per his caste. A brahmana is qualified to bathing three times a day, deity worship, reciting the Vedas, teaching, serving as a priest, taking vows, leading the life of a brahmachari (celibate) or a sannyasi (renunciant). A Kshatriya is qualified for fighting righteous wars, ruling a kingdom, protecting others, participating in works of charity, and social relief. A Vaishya is qualified for raising and protecting animals, agriculture, and commerce. A shudra is qualified to serve the deity without mantras and serving the other three castes.

A person should perform the work and follow the rules that are most becoming of his nature (caste). By honest judgment, a person can ascertain the work and lifestyle suitable to himself. If a person cannot determine his traits, a competent authority must be consulted. The caste system that is prevalent in our society today is a perverted reflection of what it once used to be. Unless the society is systematically reorganized into appropriate castes, there is little chance of India regaining its lost glory.

By desire of the Supreme Lord, the controller of all living beings, and the propounder of all rules and regulations, may there arise the perfect Caste system in India once again.

Website - www.thegaudiyatreasuresofbengal.com

Sources :

- Chaitanya Sikshamrita - Bhaktivinoda Thakura
- Brahmana and Vaishnava - Bhaktisiddhanta Saraswati Thakura

Website - www.thegaudiyatreasuresofbengal.com

Atheism vs Spirituality

Atheism vs Spirituality - What is their difference and how it can affect our lives? Well, let us discuss. In his work **'Critique of Hegel's Philosophy of Right'** Karl Marx expresses his fundamental philosophical perception of the world and life in general. After going through his work, we have come to believe that Karl Marx was fundamentally opposed to the idea of the divine. For instance, he mentions that *'criticism of religion is the prerequisite of all criticism'* and *'Religion is, indeed, the self-*

consciousness and self-esteem of man who has either not yet won through to himself, or has already lost himself again'. In this work of his, Karl Marx professes how Man should do away with religion which is *'an inverted consciousness of the world'*, in order to dispel his illusions and seek his *'true reality'*. In fact, he was of the opinion that *'The abolition of religion as the illusory happiness of the people is the demand for their real happiness'.*

Asserting that 'Religion is only the illusory Sun which revolves around man as long as he does not revolve around himself', Karl Max designates the religious pursuit of man as only a figment of his imagination. He goes a step further and expresses how -

'Religion is the sigh of the oppressed creature, the heart of a heartless world, and the soul of soulless conditions. It is the opium of the people'. His theory promoted the idea that the *'state and this society produce religion'* and that **'Man makes religion, religion does not make man'.**

Another famous socialist Friedrich Engels wrote In Ludwig Feuerbach that "*religion*

Website - www.thegaudiyatreasuresofbengal.com

arose in very primitive times from erroneous and primitive ideas of men about their own nature and that of the external world around them,... "

Vladimir Lenin, a follower of Karl Marx, appropriately summarized the thoughts of Marx in his book 'Religion' where he stated - **'Atheism is a natural and inseparable part of Marxism, of the theory and practice of scientific socialism'**

In this article, however, we are going to present our personal views on this subject. Our presentation shall deal with materialists and materialistic philosophies in general. This article is not directed towards any individual or any ideology in particular. Any views or opinions are not intended to malign any religion, ethnic group, club, organization, company, ideology or individual.

Incompatibility of Matter and Spirit - Atheism vs Spirituality

The fundamental problem with a godless philosophy is that one starts believing that matter is the only reality and hence the ultimate purpose of life. And then one starts lessening the dynamic truths of existence or profound human expressions, considering them to be nothing more than simple interactions between dead matter. Hence in most of the cases, the more exalted truths of life, remain completely elusive to the followers of such philosophies.

"The production of ideas, of conceptions, of consciousness, is at first directly interwoven with the material activity and the material intercourse of men, the language of real life. Conceiving, thinking, the mental intercourse of men, appear at this stage as the direct efflux of their material behaviour. The same applies to mental production as expressed in the language of politics, laws, morality, religion, metaphysics, etc., of a people"

(Karl Marx, The German ideology, chapter 1)

This assumption that matter is the ultimate truth of life and the interactions between matter the cause of all existence, finds its expression not only in the works of Marx and Engels, but is quite a widespread theory that is endorsed by many.

However, if we browse through the pages of ancient texts like Bhagavad Gita, we come to learn of a divine nature that constitutes the living entities. This nature is characterized as distinctively superior to dull matter.

apareyam itas tv anyam
prakritim viddhi me param
jiva-bhutam mahabaho
yayedam dharayate jagat

(Bhagavad Gita, 7.5)

Website - www.thegaudiyatreasuresofbengal.com

Apart from these, O mighty-armed (Arjuna), there is another, superior energy of Mine, that comprises the living entities, who are exploiting the resources of this inferior material nature.

The Bhagavad Gita (verse 7.4) explains that matter or material energy constitutes only of Earth, water, fire, air, ether, mind, intelligence, and false ego. But these do not constitute the vital force of living beings, who tend to Lord over the material nature. It is further explained (verse 2.17) that a living entity (both man and animals) is essentially a spirit soul who is unchangeable and indestructible. Just as the material body of a living being grows from childhood to adolescence to old age, similarly the soul passes onto another body at the time of death (verse 2.13). So despite the fact that our body changes continuously, or evolves with time, the soul however remains the same eternally. For the soul, there is no birth or death. He is unborn, timeless, primeval, and ever-existing (verse 2.20).

Website - www.thegaudiyatreasuresofbengal.com

Marx's assumption that *'Man makes religion'* is refuted in Bhagavad Gita (verse 4.1-4.2) wherein it is clearly stated how the Supreme Lord Himself is the original instructor of this imperishable spiritual knowledge *(Sri bhagavan uvaca imam vivasvate yogam proktavan aham avyayam)* that subsequently percolated down through disciplic successions and ultimately became available to the common man.

Website - www.thegaudiyatreasuresofbengal.com

It is further revealed in the scriptures how spirit and matter are incompatible and conflicting with each other. Hence it is only natural for us, spirit souls, to strive for our spiritual pursuits. One should either completely stay aloof from matter or else utilize matter only for his/her spiritual gains. Hence material activities or material occupations should only be a means to attain spiritual goals. In other words, spiritual salvation should be the prime objective of the human society. It is described how human birth is very rare and that there are 8.4 million species of life in total. It is only in this human species of life, that a living entity, gets the opportunity to use his superior intelligence and harness his inner conscience, to cultivate his spiritual ends.

But it is also explained how most of the people of this world, unfortunately, tend to get overwhelmed with matter. Consequently, these men abandon their spiritual goals and engage in gross material pursuits - that primarily involve eating, sleeping, mating, and defending, in one form or the other. These material objectives, no matter how polished they might come across, are no different from those pursued by any other

Website - www.thegaudiyatreasuresofbengal.com

animal. However, It is to be noted, that these material engagements can only provide flickering sensual pleasures that can never completely satisfy a living entity, who constitutionally hankers for unending spiritual bliss. Hence these men grow frustrated over time and keep moving from one material engagement to the other. Their journey only ends, however, when they realize their eternal spiritual nature and endeavor to attain their spiritual objectives.

It is to be surmised at this point, that the material and the spiritual viewpoints of life are entirely incompatible with each other. These philosophies not only disagree when it comes to appreciating our spiritual identities but they are complete opposites when it comes to defining life's fulfillment. Being completely ignorant of the spiritual reality of life, the materialists can never appreciate one who professes or experiences spiritual delight. These feelings, for them, are nothing but mere illusions. Karl Marx states in this regard -

"The abolition of religion as the illusory happiness of the people is

Website - www.thegaudiyatreasuresofbengal.com

the demand for their real happiness...The criticism of religion disillusions man, so that he will think, act, and fashion his reality like a man who has discarded his illusions and regained his senses, so that he will move around himself as his own true Sun. Religion is only the illusory Sun which revolves around man as long as he does not revolve around himself"

Consequently, it is quite common to come across varying philosophies or people (materialists), who labor very hard to undermine spiritual pursuits, judge spiritual emotions as hallucinations, and classify spiritual practitioners as either crazy or cheats. Their actions stem from their inability to comprehend and correlate to the existence of spirit.

That which is not 'matter' can never be approached by material pursuits or by those who reduce everything to interactions between matter. One should instead take the help of spiritual texts like Bhagavad Gita to realize the exalted stature of the highest spiritual truths.

buddhya visuddhaya yukto
dhrtyatmanam niyamya ca
sabdadin visayams tyaktva
ragadvesau vyudasya ca
vivikta sevi laghvasi
yatroparamate cittam
niruddhham yoga-sevaya
yatra chaivatmanatmanam
pasyan atmani tushyati

Website - www.thegaudiyatreasuresofbengal.com

*sukham atyantikam yat tad
buddhi grahyam atindriyam
vetti yatra na chaivayam
sthitas chalati tattvatah
yam labdhva caparam labham
manyate nadhikam tatah
yasmin sthito na duhkhena
gurunapi vichalyate
tam vidyad duhkha samyoga
viyogam yoga samjnitam
(Bhagavad Gita 6.20-23)*

In the stage of perfection called samadhi (trance), one's mind is completely restrained from material mental activities by the practice of yoga. This perfection is identified by one's ability to see the self through the uncontaminated mind and to relish and revel within the Self. In that blissful state, one is situated in boundless transcendental happiness, realized through spiritual senses. Situated thus, one never strays from the truth, and upon gaining this he thinks there is no greater gain.

Website - www.thegaudiyatreasuresofbengal.com

Being established in such an exalted position, one is never shaken, even amidst the greatest obstacle. This indeed is actual freedom from all miseries stemming from material contact.

Fallacy of Materialistic Philosophies - Atheism vs Spirituality

Materialistic philosophies that ignore the reality of spirit, cannot effectively provide solutions to the various complexities of life. Those who live by such materialistic ideologies continue entangling themselves in greater material bondage, thereby frustrating themselves even more. The reality that **'life comes from life'** and that it does not originate from dead matter baffles them and challenges their materialistic theory. Hence their tireless efforts to artificially synthesize life from chemicals in their modern labs, continue even today. However, the truth remains that Life is not a product of dead matter but instead a symptom of the soul. The vital distinction between the living and the dead

Website - www.thegaudiyatreasuresofbengal.com

body, which are chemically the same, lies in the presence and the absence of the soul respectively. Similarly, **consciousness is a symptom of the soul**. Robots, no matter how advanced they are, cannot replicate the thinking, willing and feeling of Man.

Being unable to accurately interpret the widespread evidence of NDEs (Near-death experiences), OBEs (Out of body experiences), Past Life memories, etc according to their mundane logic, they find it easier to brush them off as mere hallucinations instead.

Now, one might question why materialists do not simply accept the existence of both matter

Website - www.thegaudiyatreasuresofbengal.com

and spirit, and adopt spirituality as the ultimate goal of their life ?

The ancient scriptures explain that though the ultimate benefit of man lies in his spiritual attainment, yet sometimes he cannot let go of the affection his senses have for material objects. Harboring unlimited material desires and longing for name or fame, he works very hard and becomes bound by such fruitive activities. But his efforts only deliver flickering sensual pleasures that can never satisfy him. Growing frustrated, such materialistic people often seek the refuge of intoxication, which further degrades their consciousness and impairs their spiritual understanding. Driven by a sense of false prestige (Bhagavad Gita, verse 16.10), these men are always attracted to the world of the temporary (matter). Considering sense gratification to be the ultimate objective of human civilization, these materialistic men lead their lives in immense anxiety (Bhagavad Gita, verse 16.11-12).

The perfect Classless Society

Many of such materialistic ideologies propose the distribution of wealth in ways so that the power can be concentrated in the hands of the private owners, in the hands of the laborers or the state, etc. And in this way, they intend to reconstruct a society into an ideal one. It is to be noted, however, that no economic arrangement of this world is capable of transforming the character of an individual. If the state's leader or those in power are infested with lust and greed, there is bound to be corruption and exploitation prevailing in such a society, irrespective of its economic arrangement. These economic models simply end up transferring power from one group of corrupt individuals to another.

It must also be noted, that a Godless society which neglects the cultivation of spiritual objectives, can never attain enduring peace. Even if economic prosperity is accomplished, it can never lead to the fulfillment of its inhabitants. A living entity, who is essentially a spirit soul, can only attain lasting peace when he comes in contact with his eternal spiritual reality. No amount of money is capable of purchasing this.

Subsequently, a person who thinks that matter is the ultimate objective of life, might not restrain himself from harming others, whom he might perceive as no more valuable than a chemical compound composed of Carbon, Oxygen, and Hydrogen. In other words, such a person might be utterly unable to appreciate the gift of life. Worse, he might interpret the codes of morality, as outdated imaginary ideas formulated by weak individuals who sought refuge in religion to escape their sufferings. Hence actions that are universally considered as 'just' and 'good' might not carry much value to him. Under such circumstances, it becomes quite difficult for someone else to place their trust upon such an individual or accept him as one's leader. In short, we believe that people having a thoroughly materialistic view of life might find it difficult to establish themselves as trustworthy leaders.

Website - www.thegaudiyatreasuresofbengal.com

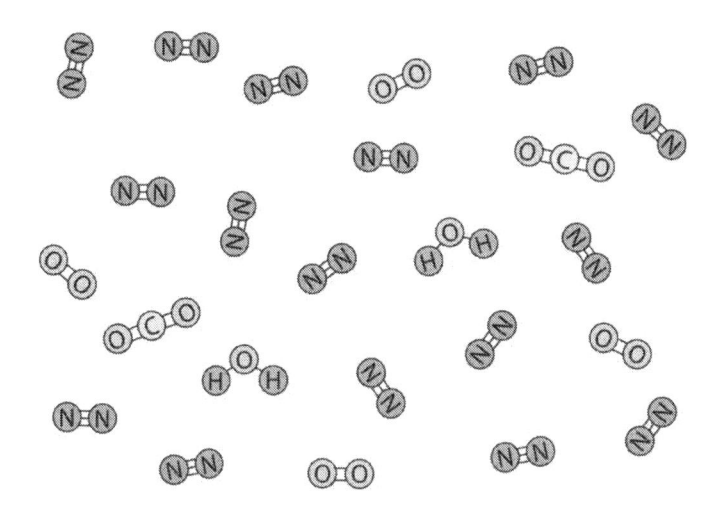

In a spiritually conscious society, however, people regard one another as a part and parcel of God. The external designations of caste, class, lineage, or how much wealth one possesses are irrelevant in such a society. On the spiritual platform, each and every living entity is respected as an equal. All of them being spirit souls. Considering themselves as servants of the Supreme Lord, the spiritualists try to serve each other and assist in each other's spiritual journey.

Hence the key to forming a perfect society characterized by universal brotherhood is not economic but instead requires a spiritual solution. A leader of such a God-centric society

Website - www.thegaudiyatreasuresofbengal.com

should uphold its spiritual heritage and bring about a holistic spiritual and economic development. Such a leader, well versed in the science of spirituality, becomes endowed with the qualities of fearlessness, charity, self-restraint, the performance of sacrifice, austerity, simplicity, non-violence, truthfulness, freedom from anger, renunciation, peacefulness, aversion to faultfinding, compassion for all living entities, freedom from covetousness, gentleness, humility, steady determination, vigor, forgiveness, fortitude, cleanliness, freedom from envy and does not crave for honor (Bhagavad Gita, verse 16.1-3). An ideal society warrants such a perfect leader.

Ending notes

Spirituality and Materialism, as we have stated before, are two incompatible and conflicting views of life. Their disagreements arise in the fundamentally opposed nature of spirit and matter itself. It is up to the individual as to which ideology he/she is willing to embrace. We must bear in mind that the reality of life remains unchanged, irrespective of how we comprehend it. Hence instead of staying loyal to any particular ideology, we must explore and adopt that which helps us understand the varying aspects of life better and makes it more meaningful. At the end of the day, the ideology of a person is bound to have a profound impact on his thoughts, actions, and decisions. An ideology, depending upon its proximity to reality, can prove to be one's best friend or his worst enemy.

Website - www.thegaudiyatreasuresofbengal.com

Depression and Anxiety - A Spiritual Solution

According to the World Health Organization, one person dies every 40 seconds by committing suicide. For each such suicide, there are at least 20 more suicide attempts. Suicide is the second leading cause of death among 15-29 years olds. Anxiety, depression, and other mental conditions that are a primary contributor to the global burden of diseases, often lead to suicide. According to WHO, more than 264 million people across the world are suffering from depression. And the number continues to grow every year. It is high time we take a close look at these pressing problems and find out a robust and effective solution. We believe that spirituality can play a pivotal role in this regard and come to the rescue of humanity.

Root cause of Anxiety and Depression - Mistaken identity of the Self

The ancient texts of Bhagavad Gita (verse 7.5) teach us that human beings, and in fact all living entities are not products of dead matter. In reality, they are constituted of a divine energy that is far superior to dull matter. The living entities are essentially spirit souls that are unborn, eternal, and ever-existing. The soul is unchangeable and indestructible. The gross body and the subtle mind are simply the coverings of the soul. Just as the material body of a living being grows from boyhood to youth to old age, similarly the soul passes onto another body at the time of death (verse 2.13). So despite the fact that our body changes continuously, or evolves with time, the soul however remains the same eternally.

Website - www.thegaudiyatreasuresofbengal.com

Man, constitutionally being a spirit soul, only finds himself in his natural element, when he focuses upon his spiritual objectives. However, if he deviates from his spiritual consciousness, he struggles to correlate with life. Forgetful of his actual spiritual identity, such a person becomes overwhelmed with the world of dead matter. His natural spiritual tendencies then get superseded by the desire to indulge in material sense gratification. Accumulating material riches or enjoying his senses grow into the primary objectives of his life.

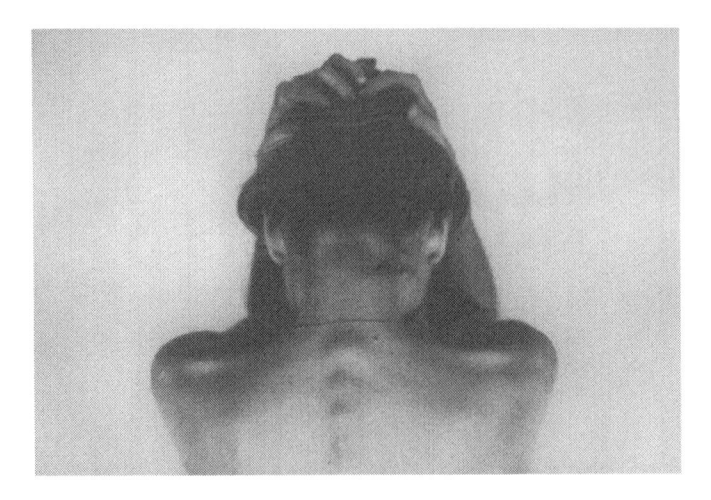

It must be understood at this point, that material things, no matter how promising, can never satisfy or provide lasting bliss to Man, who is

Website - www.thegaudiyatreasuresofbengal.com

essentially a spirit soul. Spirit and Matter are incompatible and conflicting by nature. Hence a person, suffering from a material conception of life, encircles himself with objects and objectives that can never present him with what he is truly seeking for.

Falsely identifying himself with his body and mind, such a deceived person develops an intricate web of what he labels as 'I' and 'Mine'. The world of matter is impermanent and ever-changing. Man's illusory attachments to this world of matter make him suffer a myriad of mundane happiness and distresses. Material possessions frustrate him while lack of it, makes him greedy and crave for more. The flickering sensual pleasures obtained from coming in touch with matter or material objects can never satisfy Man who is essentially seeking eternal spiritual bliss. This can only be attained, however, when Man comes to acknowledge his eternal spiritual reality and acts on that understanding to realize his spiritual goals. Therefore, we believe that the root cause of all anxieties, depressions, etc rests firmly upon this mistaken identity of the self.

Website - www.thegaudiyatreasuresofbengal.com

"What lies behind us and what lies before us are tiny as compared to what lies within us"

The Bhagavad Gita teaches that the impermanent happiness and distress that characterizes this material world are just like the various seasons that arrive and depart. They are an outcome of our sensory perceptions. And these sensations should be endured by an individual *(matra sparsas tu kaunteya sitoshna-sukha dukha dah, agamapayino nityas tams titiksasva bharata)*. We should know that just like every other thing in this world, even our sorrows are not permanent in nature. Both happiness and our distress are transitory phases of life that shall eventually pass.

But more importantly, we should recognize that the genuine cause of our sufferings is due to our false comprehension of the self. Most of us view ourselves to be nothing more than a lump of flesh and blood. If we are of material origin, then material aspirations naturally become the sole purpose of our lives. Thinking thus, we

Website - www.thegaudiyatreasuresofbengal.com

madly pursue material objectives. As a consequence, our senses seek to enjoy the impermanent material objects of this world that can only provide us with momentary flickering pleasures at best. These flickering sensual pleasures degrade our consciousness and drag us further away from our actual spiritual reality. As spirit and matter are fundamentally opposed to each other, we can either be situated in spiritual consciousness or else in material consciousness. Our illusory perceptions of 'I' and 'mine' make us enjoy and suffer as per the changing material conditions, depending on how our senses are affected by them. So though we are eternal unchangeable spiritual beings and far superior to dull matter, yet the world of the impermanent can adversely affect us, if we choose to live in this illusion.

The True Nature of the Self :

A spirit soul is always in love. Constitutionally, it is meant to love and be loved. This loving propensity of the soul is completely satisfied when it is directed towards God, the Supreme Spirit. Katha Upanishad states that the Supreme Lord is the Supreme eternal amongst all the other eternal beings. He is the fundamental conscious being among all the other conscious beings *(Nityo nityanam cetanas cetananam)*. A spirit soul is a part and parcel of the Supreme Lord and is bound to Him by love.

However, when a living entity or a spirit soul, grows forgetful of this eternal loving relationship with the supreme, he gets overwhelmed with this temporary world of matter. As the soul always seeks love, therefore when it loses touch with the divine, it turns attached to inferior material objects. However, a loving relationship with the Supreme Lord that bestows ecstatic spiritual bliss can never be substituted by love for dull matter, which only renders flickering sensual pleasures. As self-satisfaction grows far-fetched, one begins indulging in more and more sense gratification. Greater the extent of one's material entanglement, further is one's alienation from his eternal spiritual reality. Absence of divine love frustrates the soul that only hankers for eternal spiritual bliss.

Just like the Supreme Lord, a living entity is also eternal (sat), cognizant (cid), and full of bliss (ananda). The Supreme Lord is like the sun while the living entities are like sunlight. Living entities are like sparks emanating from the blazing fire of the Supreme Lord. So though the living entities are qualitatively the same with the Lord, the difference lies in their quantity. When this living entity disregards God and forgets Him, he at once comes under the influence of material nature. At that time, he develops several temporary characteristics that eclipse his eternal inclination to love the Supreme Lord. Consequently, this temporary nature of the living being overshadows his eternal blissful nature, and may even manifest itself in the form of greed, lust, envy, depression, anxiety, etc. However, it must be remembered that the original eternal nature of the living entity is never lost. It unveils itself at the appropriate time, as soon as the living being rejects his degraded material consciousness. Just as ice transforms itself into its original form of water, as soon as the freezing conditions are eliminated, similarly the living entity regains his original blissful nature as soon as he awakens his eternal relationship with the Supreme Lord.

Website - www.thegaudiyatreasuresofbengal.com

Does spirituality imply rejection of Matter ?

Now one may ask whether treading a spiritual path implies the rejection of anything that is material. One may also wonder if he/she ought to give up their dwelling in the city, let go of their phones/gadgets, and take up a residence in the forests or the mountains instead. Well, the precise answer is 'No'. When we say that one needs to give up matter, what we propose is that one abandons his/her illusory perception of 'I' and 'Mine' that originates from a material identification of the self. In other words, one needs to renounce his false material ego. Matter is not inherently harmful unless one perceives it as the very objective of his/her life.

When one realizes his/her spiritual identity and acts on that knowledge to accomplish their spiritual objectives, then one can utilize matter to achieve those ends. For example, one can use the internet to read this website article. One can buy spiritual books online, to enhance his/her spiritual understanding. One can even write books/articles, compose songs/music, etc in order to help others in their spiritual journey.

Website - www.thegaudiyatreasuresofbengal.com

When matter is utilized for spiritual goals, then it no longer remains a part of the material energy. As long as one lives in this material world, and possesses a material body, he/she requires to interact with matter. But if the purpose of that interaction is simply to derive sensual pleasures, then the particular person acts on a material platform. Instead, if one interacts with matter in order to pursue one's spiritual objectives, then one no longer entangles himself in this material predicament. So though a spiritualist interacts with matter, just like a materialist, yet there prevails a stark difference when it comes to their consciousness. A materialist puts himself at the center of his world while a spiritualist places the Supreme Lord at the center of all his actions.

One who recognizes his spiritual self will always endeavor to revive his/her eternal relationship with God. He no longer identifies with matter and possesses no interest in petty sense gratification. Instead, matter becomes a means to engage in loving devotional service of the Supreme. Such a man's involvement with this world is no longer based upon a false conception of the self and is no more motivated by sensual pleasures. He no longer traps himself in an illusory web of 'I' and 'Mine'. Engaging in selfless loving devotional service unto the Supreme, he successfully revives his eternal, blissful, and cognizant nature.

Reviving one's spiritual consciousness

The Bhagavad Gita teaches how this material complication is exceedingly difficult for a living entity to overcome *(mama maya duratyaya)*. But this incredibly challenging objective is easily accomplished by those who surrender unto the Supreme Lord and seek His divine shelter *(mam eva ye prapadyante mayam etam taranti te)*. Such a person can control his mind, transcend material nature, and even his material desires. Such a perfect devotee rejoices in boundless spiritual bliss and is not shaken even amidst the greatest of difficulties. This certainly is actual independence - freedom from all miseries (anxiety, depression, fear, etc) arising out of material contact.

Such a person identifies everything as part and parcel of the Supreme and tries to engage them in the service of the Supreme Lord. Now, one might question as to how one can take shelter of the Supreme Lord practically and revive this state of spiritual consciousness. Does it only demand an adjustment of intellectual perception or does it also require certain spiritual practices? The ancient Vedic scriptures proclaim that chanting the holy Name of the Supreme Lord is the only practical and effective means of cultivating spiritual realization (devotion) in this present day and age *(Harer nama harer nama harer namaiva kevalam kalau nasthyeva nasthyeva nasthyeva gathir anyatha - Brhan Naradiya Purana)*. Nothing else is as powerful. Love of the Supreme Lord is not something that can be achieved artificially from an external source. It is eternally existing within the hearts of all living entities. When the heart is purified by the process of regular hearing and chanting the holy names, glories of the Supreme Lord, this eternal love awakens and reveals itself once more *(nitya-siddha Krishna-prema 'sadhya' kabhu naya, sravanadi suddha chitte karaye udaya- Chaitanya Charitamrta)*.

Website - www.thegaudiyatreasuresofbengal.com

Bhakti Yoga and Ashtanga Yoga

(The below is adapted from Srila Bhaktivinoda Thakura's 'Prema Pradipa' and talks in length about the two Types of Yoga - Bhakti Yoga and Ashtanga Yoga. The following is an excerpt of the enlightening conversation between Sri Premadasa babaji and an Ashtanga Yogi)

*yamadaibhir yoga pathaih
kama-lobha hato muhuh
mukunda-sevaya yadvat
tathatmaddha na samyati
(Srimad Bhagavatam, 1.6.35)*

Website - www.thegaudiyatreasuresofbengal.com

Though it is true that by exercising restraint of the senses by the yoga system one can get respite from the disturbances of desire and lust, yet this is not sufficient to give satisfaction to the soul, for this is derived from devotional service unto the Supreme Lord.

Citing the above verse, Sri Premadasa Babaji added that Yama, Niyama, asana, Pranayama, pratyahara, dhyana, Dharana, and samadhi constitute the process of Ashtanga Yoga. It is true that by practicing them one achieves peace. However in certain circumstances, the practitioner, being overwhelmed with lust and greed, may indulge himself in relishing some trivial intermediary results. Thus instead of persevering for the ultimate objective of peace, he may fall down and get derailed from his Yogic practice. But in the process of rendering devotional service unto Sri Krishna, there is no chance of receiving any intermediary results. Hence a servant of Lord Krishna, definitely obtains his desired peace.

In this assembly was present an 'Ashtanga Yogi', who could not agree with Sri Premadasa Babaji completely. Although this Ashtanga Yogi was also a Vaishnava, yet he had practiced the process of Ashtanga Yoga for many years and had achieved perfection in this path. As a consequence he prioritized the process of Ashtanga Yoga over the ninefold processes of bhakti yoga.

This yogi exclaimed," Babaji, Do not belittle the process of Ashtanga yoga. The yogis, despite living for so long, can go without food or sleep for days. Is it possible for you to execute devotional service as sincerely and as intensely as they can? Therefore you should understand that the path of Yoga is superior to that of arcana (worship).

Vaishnavas are naturally disinclined to engage themselves in confronting debates. However no one in the assembly liked the yogi-Vaishnava's statement minimizing the importance of bhakti yoga over Ashtanga yoga. But everyone stayed silent. The yogi felt embarrassed and requested Premadasa Babaji to state his conclusion on this subject. Premadasa Babaji was initially

Website - www.thegaudiyatreasuresofbengal.com

disinclined to enter into the argument. However, when the yogi repeatedly assured him that he would accept his conclusion, the Babaji spoke as follows -

Types of Yoga - Superiority of Bhakti Yoga

The ultimate objective of both Yoga practice and devotional service is Bhagavan (the Supreme Personality of Godhead) who is the worshipable object of all living entities. The living entities can broadly be classified into two - pure and conditioned. Those living beings who have no connection with and are completely transcendental to material nature are pure living entities. While those who are entangled in material nature are conditioned living beings. The 'Sadhaka' or the 'practitioner' is a conditioned living entity while the pure living entity has nothing to practice (for he is already perfect). The difference between the two is that a pure living entity is already situated in his constitutional position (as a servant of the Lord); therefore his actions are completely spiritual and his nature is pure bliss.

On the other hand, a conditioned living being is entangled in material nature and accepts materially designated duties which are of mixed material and spiritual qualities.

Rejecting such materially designated duties and accepting pure duties based upon one's constitutional position, is termed as liberation. Achieving the pure love of God and achieving liberation cannot be two different things. The deliverance sought by yogic practice is the same as the love of Godhead achieved by practicing devotional service. Therefore the ultimate objective of both these practices is the same. It is for this reason that the Vedic scriptures often describe the great devotee Sukadeva Goswami as a Maha-yogi while the foremost Yogi Lord Shiva is often depicted as a great devotee.

Website - www.thegaudiyatreasuresofbengal.com

The principal difference between the paths of Yoga and devotional service is that by strictly practicing Yoga, when one attains samadhi by giving up his temporary designations, he achieves his constitutional position -thereby awakening Prema (pure love of God). The only fear is that it takes a significant amount of time to achieve this ultimate goal, through the process of Ashtanga Yoga. Therefore it is quite probable for the practitioner to get bewildered and overwhelmed by some trivial intermediary by-products and fall down before achieving perfection.

On the other hand, the process of devotional service only deals with Prema (pure love of God). Devotional service is simply the cultivation of this science of love. When all activities in a process are geared towards achieving the ultimate result, there is no fear of ending up with any insignificant trivial results. The means are the end and the end are the means. Therefore the path of devotional service is simpler as compared to Ashtanga Yoga and should be accepted by all.

The path of Ashtanga Yoga is full of impediments :

The control over material nature that is gained by the practice of Yoga is only a temporary result. This often leads to further difficulties. Firstly while practicing Yama and Niyama, the fruit of religiosity is awakened. Being overwhelmed with this trivial result, one might take pleasure in being renowned as being religious-minded without further endeavoring to achieve Prema (love of God), the ultimate objective.

Secondly, by practicing asana and pranayama for a prolonged time, one might obtain a long life free from diseases. But if this long life is devoid of Prema (love of God), then it becomes a source of trouble.

By practicing Yoga, one gains control of his senses by withdrawing them (pratyahara). However, if one does not develop the love of God in the process, then the subsequent renunciation manifested by such a Sadhaka is only dry and trivial. Accepting or rejecting anything for the ultimate spiritual objective is evenly fruitful. However, if the ultimate objective is missing, then such meaningless renunciation only ends up making one stonehearted.

During Dhyana, Dharana, and Samadhi if one can remove material thoughts but is unable to evoke divine love (Prema), then such a living entity loses his individuality. If the understanding of 'I am Brahman' does not result in invoking the pure love of God, then it destroys one's existence or individuality.

Hence please consider that though the ultimate objective of Yoga is wonderful, yet its path is full of impediments. On the other hand the process of devotional service is free from such complications. Then addressing the yogi, Sri Premadasa Babaji exclaimed, 'You are a Vaishnava and a Yogi. Hence you shall be able to understand my words without any bias'. Even before the babaji had finished, the assembled Vaishnavas highly appreciated his excellent response.

Types of Yoga - The Yogi responds :

The Yogi Babaji responded by saying, 'Babaji, your conclusions are wonderful but I have something to say in this regard. Before practicing Ashtanga Yoga, I had practiced the nine limbs of devotional service, beginning with hearing and chanting. But frankly, my senses were so strong that practically in every action, I sought out sense gratification. I could not untangle my heart from the false designations as described in Vaishnava instructions on conjugal rasa. Only after I practiced Pratyahara (withdrew my senses through Ashtanga Yoga), could I relish the spiritual essence of conjugal rasa. Now, I do not desire for sense gratification anymore. There is a provision for practicing

Pranayama in Arcana (worship). I feel that this practice has been suggested as pratyahara or withdrawing one's senses in bhakti yoga. Therefore I feel that Yogic practices are also essential'.

Bhakti Yoga cannot be practiced as a dry selfish fruitive ritual :

Sri Premadasa babaji thought about the Yogi's statements for a while. Then he replied as follows -

'Babaji, you are blessed for you did not forget rasa-tattva (devotional mellows) even while exercising 'Pratyahara' (withdrawal of senses). In most cases, dry speculation and dry practices cause fall down from one's spiritual path. It is because the soul, being full of bliss, cannot appreciate dryness. The soul is always in love. Therefore if it loses touch with the divine, then it gets attached to the inferior material objects. As self-satisfaction grows far-fetched, one begins indulging in sense gratification. When this soul, which is the Lord of the senses, happens to come in contact with its eternal Rasa, its spontaneous attraction awakens and its material desire diminishes. Bhakti Yoga or the path of devotion is nothing but the discussions of love for the Supreme Lord. The more one is attached to it, the lesser he entangles himself in sense gratification.

I believe, when you practiced devotional service, you had not received the association of pure devotees. You have executed the ninefold processes of devotional service as if they were some dry fruitive selfish rituals. As a consequence, you did not obtain even a drop of transcendental bliss. And it is for this reason that the urge to satisfy your senses increased. Under these circumstances, there is a chance of getting some benefit by practicing Yoga. The practicing devotee must relish the mellows of devotion in the association of other devotees. Even though a devotee experiences all kinds of material sense gratification, this enjoyment does not affect him or lead to a craving for more enjoyment. Sense enjoyment is the primary cause of devotees' rejecting the desire for material enjoyment'.

The Yogi revealed that he did not previously know about this matter and expressed his gratitude for Sri Premadasa Babaji's words.

27 facts of Life

Life as we know it is a wonderful opportunity to recognize our true potentials and utilize them to help us and others perfect their existence. Being accustomed to the bondage of material existence, it is almost impossible for one to decipher the meaning of life on his own. Tired of suffering the pangs of material miseries, or being very inquisitive to reach the ultimate truth, a few fortunate souls might become the recipient of divine mercy. Life grows beautiful and the facts of life are interpreted very differently, once the seeds of devotion are rooted in one's heart. The following article is an

Website - www.thegaudiyatreasuresofbengal.com

interpretation of the colorful panorama of life from the viewpoint of the philosophy of Gaudiya Vaishnavism.

#1 There are three fundamental entities that exist - God, living beings (jiva), and the dead. An entity that does not possess consciousness or the power of will can be classified as dead. Hence water, fire, earth, ether, wind, etc can be classified as dead matter. On the other hand, Man, animals, birds, etc can be classified as living entities as they are conscious and possess the ability of thinking and willing to a varying degree.

Bhumir apo 'nala vayu kham mano
buddhir eva ca
Ahankara itiyam me bhinna
prakritir astadha

(Bhagavad Gita 7.4)

-

(Lord Krishna said) Earth, water, fire, ether, mind, intelligence and false ego - these constitute my eight separate material energies.

Website - www.thegaudiyatreasuresofbengal.com

Apareyam itas tv anyam prakrtim viddhi me paramJiva bhutan maha baho yayedam dharyate jagat

(Bhagavad Gita 7.5)

-

(Lord Krishna continued) O mighty-armed Arjuna, besides these, there is another, superior energy of Mine, which comprises the living entities who are exploiting the reserves of this material world.

#2 Of all the conscious beings, Man is the most conscious, and his ability of thinking, willing, and feeling far surpasses the other living entities.

*durlabha manava-janma labhiya samsare
Krishna na bhajinu-dukha kahibo kahare
(Song - Durlabha manava janma)*

-

Website - www.thegaudiyatreasuresofbengal.com

The human form of life is the rarest opportunity for attaining spiritual perfection. But now I am lamenting, because I've somehow or other been born with such an opportunity, but I have wasted it by never worshiping Lord Krishna, the Supreme Personality of Godhead. Oh, to whom shall I relate the tale of this misery?

#3 God is the creator of both the conscious and the dead. He is the Supreme conscious being and complete in all respects. He is the ultimate controller and the supreme cause of all causes.

He dwells in the spiritual world, which is separate from this world of dead matter. It is by His divine will that this creation survives and remains functional.

*etad-yonini bhutani sarvanity
upadharaya
aham kritsnasya jagata prabhavah
pralayas tatha*

(Bhagavad Gita 7.6)

Website - www.thegaudiyatreasuresofbengal.com

All created beings have their source in these two kinds of energies (spiritual and material). Of all that is material and all that is spiritual in this world, know for certain that I am both the origin and the dissolution.

#4 God is not formless. God possesses a form too but He is not trapped in a body of dead matter like us. As a result, He cannot be perceived by our gross material senses. That is why the revealed scriptures state that God is 'Nirakara' or without any form. The truth is that God does possess a form but that form is not material.

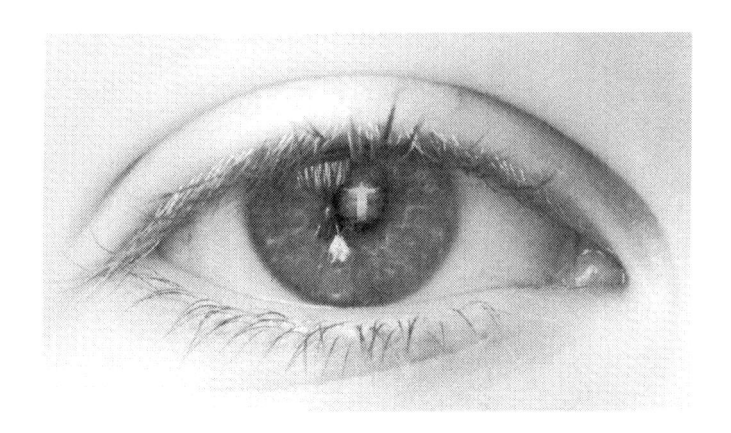

#5 All living entities, the conscious beings, are essentially spirit souls. We, the living entities of this world (humans, birds, animals, trees, etc) are spiritual beings trapped in bodies of dead matter. The Supreme Lord, however, possesses a spiritual body that is free from any traces or contaminations of matter. In other words, His form is entirely spiritual.

*isvarah paramah Krishna
Sac-cid-ananda-vigrahah
anadir adir govindah
sarva-karana-karanam*

(Brahma Samhita)

-

Krishna who is also known as Govinda (controller of our senses) is the Supreme Personality of Godhead. He has an eternal blissful spiritual body. He is the origin of all. He has no origin. He is the prime cause of all causes.

#6 Hence the Supreme Lord cannot be observed with material senses, but only through eyes anointed with devotion.

*Premanjana-cchurita-bhakti-vilocanena
santah sadaiva hrdayesu vilokayanti
yam syamasundaram acintya-guna-svarupam
govindam adi-purusam tam aham bhajami*

(Brahma Samhita 5.38)

-

I worship Govinda, the primeval Lord, who is Shyamasundara Krsna Himself, possessing inconceivable innumerable qualities, and whom the pure devotees see in their heart of hearts with the eye of devotion tinged with the salve of love.

#7 Just like a blind person cannot observe the rays of the sun, similarly, a few unfortunate people of this world disprove the existence of

God simply because they cannot perceive Him physically with their material eyes.

naham prakasah sarvasya yoga-maya-samavritah

mudho 'yam nabhijanati loko mam ajam avyayam

(Bhagavad Gita 7.25)

-

(Lord Krishna said) I am never manifest to the foolish and unintelligent. For them I am covered by My internal energy (yoga-maya), and therefore they do not know that I am unborn and infallible.

Aprakrta vastu nahe prakrta gochara
Vede puranete ei kahe nirantara

(Chaitanya Charitamrita 9.194)

-

Website - www.thegaudiyatreasuresofbengal.com

Spiritual substance is never within the scope and jurisdiction of the material interpretation. Vedas and the Puranas mention this repeatedly.

#8 The spiritual world (Vaikuntha) is situated far beyond the realm of matter. It is eternal, blissful, spiritual, and free from faults of material contamination. It cannot be observed with material eyes or perceived by our subtle minds. The spiritual world is inconceivable (Achintya) to us imperfect embodied beings. It is over here that the Supreme Lord resides along with His eternal associates.

*na tad bhasayate suryo na sasanko na pavakah
yad gatva na nivartante tad dhama paramam mama*

(Bhagavad Gita 15.6)

-

That supreme abode of Mine is not illumined by the sun or moon, nor by fire or electricity. Those who attain it never return to this material world.

#9 The whole purpose of our existence is to render loving devotional service unto the Supreme Lord, recognizing Him to be our ever well-wisher and our eternal object of love. One who knows this and awakens his/her eternal loving propensity for the Supreme Lord is awarded the opportunity to reside in the spiritual world and engage in loving service of the Supreme Lord. The spiritual world is free from miseries. It is eternal, full of knowledge, and bliss.

*Naham vipro na ca nara patir
Napi vaisyo na sudro
Naham varni na ca griha patir
No vanastho yatir va
Kintu prodyan nikhila paramananda purnamritabdher
Gopi bhartuh pada kamalayor dasa dasanudasah*

(Chaitanya Charaitamrita, Madhya, 13.80)

-

Website - www.thegaudiyatreasuresofbengal.com

I am not a brahmana, nor a Kshatriya. I am not a vaisya nor a shudra. Nor am I a brahmachari, a householder, a vanaprastha, or a sannyasi. I identify Myself only as the servant of the servant of the servant of the lotus feet of Lord Krishna, the maintainer of the gopis. He is like an ocean of nectar and is the cause of universal transcendental bliss. He is always existing in brilliance.

(Lord Chaitanya to Lord Jagannatha)

#10 The material world that we live in is temporary and full of miseries. It is tormented by the problems of birth, disease, old age, and death that are all sources of trouble for the embodied soul. The soul is subjected to a lot of miseries in the mother's womb where it is forced to lie in a constrained position and endure worm bites for ten long months. After taking birth, one has to tirelessly endeavor for food, shelter, and security, failing which one can be plunged into more difficulties. Natural disasters, diseases, and disputes with others cause added pain to the living entity. In short, there is nothing called unadulterated happiness in this material world. The short gap of time, when one is devoid of material miseries, is falsely claimed to be 'happiness' by the illusioned living entity.

mam upetya punar janma
duhkhalayam asasvatam
napnuvanti mahatmanah
samsiddhim paramam gatah

(Bhagavad Gita 8.15)

-

After attaining Me, the great souls, who are yogis engaged in devotional service, never return to this temporary world, which is full of miseries, because they have achieved the highest perfection.

#11 Out of 8.4 million species of life, a human being is the most conscious and is perfectly equipped to attain complete spiritual realization. Hence one should not waste the precious human form of life and instead utilize it for God-realization from an early age. Death is unpredictable and can approach us at any moment.

*vasamsi jirnani yatha vihaya navani
grihnati naro parani*

*tatha sarirani vihaya jirnany anyani
samyati navani dehi*

(Bhagavad Gita 2.22)

-

As a person puts on new clothes, giving up old ones, the soul similarly accepts new material bodies, giving up the old and useless ones.

#12 The state of consciousness one quits his/her body during death decides the destination of the concerned soul. The actions performed during one's lifetime have the greatest impact on one's consciousness. Depending upon one's state of consciousness at the time of death one can be sent to the abode of ghosts/spirits, sent to suffer in hell, united with one's ancestors, sent to the heavens to enjoy celestial pleasures, or completely relieved of any material designations and sent back home to the spiritual world, where one can reunite with his/her eternal master.

yam yam vapi smaran bhavam
tyajaty ante kalevaram
tam tam evaiti kaunteya
sada tad-bhava-bhavitah

(Bhagavad Gita 8.6)

-

Whatever state of being one remembers at the time of quitting his/her body, that state he will attain without fail (in his next life)

#13 Unless one is freed from material designations, one continues to suffer in this material world, transmigrating from one body to the next. All embodied living entities starting from demigods enjoying in heaven to small ants of this world are subject to birth, disease, old age, and death.

Website - www.thegaudiyatreasuresofbengal.com

#14 Fear, hope, sense of duty, and natural attraction (love) towards the Supreme Lord are the most noticeable factors initially driving one to serve God. As one practices devotion, the abovementioned factors of fear, hope, and duty gradually fade away and make way for the spontaneous pure love for God. Devotional life is a reservoir of unadulterated bliss and one who tastes it can no longer be content with any material pleasures or circumstances.

Premera svabhave kare citta tanu kshobha
Krishnera charana praptye upajaye lobha

(Chaitanya Charitamrita 7.87)

Website - www.thegaudiyatreasuresofbengal.com

Love of God (Prema) by its very nature induces transcendental symptoms in one's body and makes one more and more greedy to attain the shelter of the Lord's lotus feet.

#15 Spontaneous love or 'Raga' is the ideal way of rendering devotional service unto God. Awakening of this spontaneous relationship is the success of one's life. This relationship between the Supreme Lord and the living entity is an eternal truth, forgetting which the living entity subjects himself/herself to countless material miseries.

Krishnera charane haya yadi anuraga
Krishna vinu anyatra tara nahi rahe raga

(Chaitanya Charitamrita, Adi, 7.143)

-

If one develops his love of Godhead and grows attached to the lotus feet of Krishna, the Supreme Lord, then he gradually loses his affection for everything else.

#16 Devotion unto God driven by fear, hope, or duty cannot be considered pure. Devotees practicing them are inferior to those who render devotional service unto God driven by spontaneous love (Raga). However, as discussed before, hope, fear, and duty make way for spontaneous love, as one gradually evolves in his/her devotional life.

Tantra seva vina jivera na yaya samsara
Tanhara charana priti - purusartha sara
Moksadi ananda yara nahe eka kana
Purnananda prapti tanra charana sevana

(Chaitanya Charitamrita, Madhya, 18.194-195)

-

No conditioned soul can get out of material bondage without serving the Supreme Personality of Godhead. Loving His lotus feet is the ultimate goal of life. The joy of liberation, whereby one merges into the Lord's existence cannot even be compared to a fragment of the transcendental bliss obtained by serving the Supreme Lord's lotus feet.

#17 If we examine the life and history of people living in various parts of the world, we shall come to realize that faith in God is universal and a natural characteristic of people in general. Even the uncivilized tribes living in the forest, worship trees, rivers, mountains, etc, and exhibit their reverence towards the divine.

Jivera svarupa haya - Krishnera nitya dasa
Krishnera tathastha sakti bhedabheda prakash

(Chaitanya Charitamrita, Madhya, 20.108)

-

It is the living entity's constitutional position to be an eternal servant of Krishna. He is the marginal energy (tathastha sakti) of Krishna and a manifestation of being simultaneously one with and different from the Supreme Lord.

#18 No two personalities are the same. Hence culture, actions, customs, manners, characteristics, lifestyles of people vary in different parts of the world. Hence although faith and worship of God is a universal practice, it is followed differently by different people.

#19 As long as the principal goal is to serve and render devotion unto the Supreme Lord, the secondary differences between people and their ways of worship do not matter. Hence one should be very careful in not criticizing other devotees who may possess a different style of worshiping the same Supreme Lord.

Yei bhaje sei bada, abhakta hina chhara
Krishna bhajane nahi jati-kuladi-vichara

(Chaitanya Charitamrita, Aunty, 4.67)

-

Anyone who takes to devotional service is exalted, whereas a non-devotee is always condemned and fallen. Therefore in the discharge of devotional service towards the Supreme Lord, there is no consideration of caste, class, or one's family lineage.

#20 Different people might be loyal followers of different religious teachers. Their ways of worshiping God might be different or they might call upon God with a different name. One should understand however that the ultimate goal of all religious practices is attaining love of God. Hence, one should strictly avoid criticizing other religious practices or harboring any rivalry against each other. One should always consider other religious practices as different ways of worshipping the same Supreme Lord.

#21 If one harbors hate, resentment, or enviousness towards other religious groups, it must be assumed that such a person does not value his supreme interest or love the Supreme Lord more than he is inclined in confronting others.

#22 As stated earlier, the petty differences between various religious groups are insignificant, as long attaining the love of God is the principal goal. At the same time, it should be recorded that a particular religious practice must be free from faults like atheism, speculation, materialism, voidism, etc. In other words, a philosophy or a religious practice that serves in pushing a soul away from its natural tendency to love the Supreme Lord must be rejected. Such philosophies or religious practices do not help the soul unite with the Supersoul and are hence not above criticism.

Bhakti siddhanta viruddha ,ara rasabhasa
Sunite na haya prabhura chittera ullasa
(Chaitanya Charitamrita, Madhya, 10.113)

Website - www.thegaudiyatreasuresofbengal.com

Sri Chaitanya Mahaprabhu was never pleased to listen to books or verses that are opposed to conclusive statements of devotional service. The Lord did not like hearing rasabhasa, the overlapping of transcendental mellows.

#23 In order to bloom, Love requires a lover and an object of love. Without them, love holds no identity. Likewise, the living entity is the lover and God is the ultimate object of his eternal love.

#24 Once this love blossoms and turns spontaneous, the Supreme Lord is completely revealed unto the living entity. As this divine love grows, the impersonal conception of God is replaced with a personal one. The living entity realizes that God is a person possessing a set of qualities and fully capable of reciprocating personally.

Website - www.thegaudiyatreasuresofbengal.com

#25 As this divine love evolves further, awe and reverence for the all-powerful and all-opulent Supreme Lord give way to an intense attraction and attachment for His sweetness, magnanimity, and His unlimited other qualities. Such a devotee now no longer fears the Lord or worships Him for any material benedictions. Instead, he worships the Lord for he cannot help but associate with his object of eternal love.

Maryada haite koti sukha sneha acharane
Paramananda haya yara nama-sravane

(Chaitanya Charitamrita, Madhya, 10.140)

Website - www.thegaudiyatreasuresofbengal.com

Dealing affectionately with the Supreme Personality of Godhead is many millions of times more ecstatic than dealing with Him in awe and veneration. Simply by hearing the holy name of the Lord, the devotee is merged in transcendental bliss.

#26 Such a devotee can control his mind, transcend material nature, and even his material desires. Such a perfect devotee rejoices in boundless spiritual bliss and is not shaken even amidst the greatest of difficulties. This certainly is actual independence - freedom from all miseries arising out of material contact. Such a person identifies everything as part and parcel of the Supreme and tries to engage them in the service of the Supreme Lord.

Taiche bhakti phale Krishne prema upajaye
Preme Krishna-svada haile bhavna nasha paya
Daridrya nasha, bhava kshaya - premera 'phala' naya

Website - www.thegaudiyatreasuresofbengal.com

Prema sukha bhoga - mukhya prayojana haya

(Chaitanya Charitamrita, Madhya, 20.141-142)

-

As a result of devotional service unto Lord Krishna, one's dormant love for Krishna awakens. When one is so situated that he can taste the association of Lord Krishna, his material existence, the repetition of birth and death reaches an end. The goal of love of Godhead is not to grow materially rich or free from material bondage. the real goal is to be situated in devotional service to the Lord and to enjoy transcendental bliss.

#27 The ancient Vedic scriptures proclaim that chanting the holy Name of the Supreme Lord is the only practical and effective means of cultivating spiritual realization (devotion) in this present day and age *(Harer nama harer nama harer namaiva kevalam kalau nasthyeva*

Website - www.thegaudiyatreasuresofbengal.com

nasthyeva nasthyeva gathir anyatha - Brhan Naradiya Purana). Nothing else is as powerful. Love of the Supreme Lord is not something that can be achieved artificially from an external source. It is eternally existing within the hearts of all living entities. When the heart is purified by the process of regular hearing and chanting the holy names, glories of the Supreme Lord, this eternal love awakens and reveals itself once more.

*nitya-siddha Krishna-prema
'sadhya' kabhu naya,
sravanadi suddha chitte karaye
udaya*

(Chaitanya Charitamrta, Madhya, 22.107)

-

Pure love for Krishna is eternally established in the hearts of the living entities. It is not something to be gained from an external source. When one's heart is purified by the regular hearing and chanting of Krishna's holy name and glories, this love naturally awakens.

15 Benefits of Chanting Hare Krishna Mahamantra | Glories of Hare Krishna Mahamantra

All glories to Sri Krishna Sankirtanam! All glories to the Hare Krishna Mahamantra! Realize the benefits of chanting the Hare Krishna Mahamantra !!!

Website - www.thegaudiyatreasuresofbengal.com

#1 In this age of Kali the only means of spiritual salvation is the chanting of Krishna's holy name and glories (Sri-Krishna-Kirtana). No other activity surpasses the effectiveness of this.

*harer-nama harer-nama harer-namaiva kevalam
kalau nasty-eva nasty-eva nasty-eva gatir anyatha*

(Brhad Naradiya Purana)

-

In this age of Kali the only means of deliverance is chanting of the holy name of Lord Hari. There is no other way. There is no other way. There is no other way.

#2 Chanting the Holy name of Lord Hari destroys all sins

Sri Chaitanya Mahaprabhu said:

One of the features of the Holy name is that it destroys all sins. First of all, hear about this subject based on evidence from the scriptures.

Take note of the sinner Ajamila who had chanted the holy name 'Narayana', lying helplessly (upon his deathbed). He immediately became absolved of the innumerable sins that he had committed over millions of his births.

*ayam hi krta-nirveso janma-koty-amhasam api
yad vyajahara vivaso nama svasty-ayanam
hareh*

(Srimad Bhagavatam, 6.2.7)

(The Vishnu-Dutas said) Ajamila has already atoned for all his sinful actions. Indeed, he has atoned not only for sins performed in this life but also for those he had performed in millions of lives. It is because he had chanted the holy name of Narayana in a helpless condition.

#3 Religious rites and vows are insignificant in comparison to chanting the Holy Name of Hari

Sri Chaitanya Mahaprabhu explained :

The religious rites like 'Chandrayan Vrata' as mentioned in the scriptures do not completely eradicate the sins of a sinner. The chanting of Lord Hari's holy Name just once, however, delivers the sinner of all his sins.

*na niskrtair uditair brahma vadibhis
tatha visuddhyaty-aghavan vratadibhih
yatha harer nama-padair udahrtais
tad uttamahsloka-gunopalambhakam*

(Srimad Bhagavatam, 6.2.11)

-

(Vishnu-Dutas said) By following the Vedic ritualistic ceremonies or undergoing atonement, sinful men do not become as purified as by chanting the holy name of Lord Hari. The chanting of the holy Name reminds one of the Lord's qualities.

Website - www.thegaudiyatreasuresofbengal.com

#4 One who chants the holy name of Lord Hari attains Vaikuntha

If one chants the holy name of Krishna or Hari indirectly, jokingly, for entertainment or even neglectfully - then this namabhasa (impure but offenseless chanting of the Holy Name) will destroy his innumerable sins and enable him to enter into Vaikuntha(the spiritual world) overstepping the jurisdiction of Yamadutas (attendants of Yamaraja).

sanketyam parihasyam va stobham helanam eva va
vaikuntha-nama-grahanam-asesagha-haram viduh

(Srimad Bhagavatam, 6.2.14)

-

(Vishnu-dutas said) Even if one chants the holy name of the Lord indirectly, jokingly, for entertainment, or even neglectfully, one is immediately freed from the reactions of unlimited sins. This is accepted by all the learned transcendentalists.

Yamaraja never torments those who helplessly and submissively call out the names of Krishna, Hari or Narayana after having fallen, slipped, been broken, bitten, burnt or having suffered an injury.

patitah skhalito bhagnah sandastas tapta ahatah
harir-ity-avashenaha puman-narhati yatanah
(Srimad Bhagavatm, 6.2.15)

-

(Vishnu-dutas said) If one chants the holy name of Hari and then dies because of an accidental misfortune, such as falling, slipping, suffering broken body, being bitten, burnt, or being injured, then one is immediately absolved from

Website - www.thegaudiyatreasuresofbengal.com

having to enter hellish life, even though he is sinful.

#5 Chanting absolves sins of the past as well as sins that are yet to fructify

The Holy Name of the Lord quickly nullifies the reactions to one's present sins, sins associated with one's previous lives, and sins that shall fructify in the future. The living entity has no friend in his life other than the Holy Name of the Supreme Lord.

vartamanas tu yat papam yadbhutam yad-bhavishyati

tat sarvam nirdahatyasu govinda-kirtananalah

(Laghu Bhagavata)

-

The fire of chanting of Lord Govinda's Name quickly burns away the reactions to sinful activities that have accumulated not only in this life but over many past lives and even those which are yet to ripen in the future.

Even those who offend and commit sins against the virtuous people of this world attain deliverance by chanting the Holy Name of the Supreme Lord.

sada droha-paro yas tu sajjananam mahitale

jayate pabano dhanyo harer-namanukirtanat

(Laghu Bhagavata)

-

An offense committed against a saintly person is a grave violation and can only be atoned by chanting the Holy Name of the Lord.

#6 The Holy name cures all diseases

All the Vedic scriptures sing that the holy name of the Supreme Lord can cure all diseases.

Achyutananda-govinda-namochcharana-bhisitah
nasyanti sakala rogah satyam satyam vadamy aham

(Brhan Naradiya Purana)

-

This is the Truth! This is the Truth! Chanting the Names 'Achyutananda' and 'Govinda' causes diseases to die out of fear.

Website - www.thegaudiyatreasuresofbengal.com

#7 The Holy Name transforms the greatest sinners into the most glorious saints

*mahapataka-yukto pi
kirtayan manisam harim
suddhantahkarano bhutva
jayate pamkti-pavanah*

(Brahmanda Purana)

-

By chanting the Holy Name of the Lord day and night, even the greatest sinner is purified and is transformed into a saint who can purify others by his association.

Website - www.thegaudiyatreasuresofbengal.com

#8 Chanting the Holy name dispels fear and punishments

The Fear of terrible diseases or the fear of being punished by the King is driven away by chanting the Holy Name of Narayana.

> *Mahavyadhi-samach-chhanno*
> *Raja-vadhopapiditah*
> *narayaneti sankirtya*
> *niratanko bhaven narah*
>
> (Vahni Purana)

-

Living beings who are troubled with terrible diseases or oppressed by kings grow fearless by chanting the Holy Name of Narayana.

All kinds of diseases, sufferings, along with troubles and calamities are destroyed by chanting the Holy Name of Lord Hari.

> *sarva-roga-upasamanam sarvopadrava-*
> *nasanam*
> *santidam sarva aristanam harer nama*
> *anukirtanam*

(Brhad Vishnu Purana)

-

Chanting the Holy Name of the Supreme Lord Hari heals all diseases, ends all troubles and subdues all disasters.

Just as the mighty wind scatters the clouds, and the rising sun certainly dissipates the darkness - similarly the Holy Name of the Lord drives away the calamities that torment the living beings on the strength of its potency. These are the words of Vyasadeva.

sankirtyamano bhagavan anantah
srutanubhavo vyasanam hi pumsam
pravisya cittam vidhunoty asesam
yatha tamo 'rko 'bhram ivati vatah
(Srimad Bhagavatm, 12.12.48)

-

When a living entity chants about the Infinite Supreme Personality of Godhead, or hears about His prowess, the Lord enters their hearts and cleanses away their misfortunes, just as the sun dispels the darkness or as a powerful wind scatters the clouds.

#9 Chanting the Holy name of Lord Hari with faith counteracts the adverse ill-effects of Kali Yuga

In this dark age of Kali, sincere devotees should give up all other shelters and take exclusive shelter of the Holy Name of Lord Hari.

Chanting the Holy Names of 'Hari', 'Keshava', 'Govinda', 'Vasudeva', 'Jagan-Maya' fulfills one's heart with great bliss.

One who chants the Holy Name of the Supreme Lord with unflinching faith is not affected by the reverses of Kali Yuga and his heart stays eternally pure.

Website - www.thegaudiyatreasuresofbengal.com

*harinama-para ye ca ghore kali-yuge narah
te eva krtakrtyasca na kalir badhate hi tan
hare keshava govinda vasudeva jaganmaya
itirayanti ye nityam na hi tan badhate kalih*

(Brhan Naradiya Purana)

-

Living beings who devote themselves to the chanting of the Holy Names of the Supreme Lord Hari are not affected by the reverses of Kali Yuga. Chanting the Holy Names 'Hari', 'Keshava', 'Govinda', 'Vasudeva', 'Jagan-Maya' ,one overcomes the hindrances posed by Kali Yuga.

#10 Chanting the Holy name of Lord Hari is superior to the study of all 4 Vedas

Website - www.thegaudiyatreasuresofbengal.com

The Holy Name of the Supreme Lord is superior to all the Vedas. One who doubts this never attains any good fortune.

'Pranava' or 'Om' is another Name of Krishna, and it is from this sound, spoken first by Brahma, that the Vedas had originated. Essentially these two (Krishna's name and the Vedas) have no distinction. Hence one who constantly chants the Holy names of Lord Hari has already recited the Rig, Yajur, Sama and Atharva Vedas.

rig-vedo hi yajur-vedah sama-vedo py atharvanah
adhitas tena yenoktam haririty akshara dvayam

(Vishnu Dharma Purana)

-

Those who have chanted the two syllables 'Hari' have certainly studied the Rig, Yajur, Sama and Atharva Vedas.

What is the use of studying the Rig, Yajur, Sama and Atharva Veda? Just chant the holy name of 'Govinda'.

ma richo ma yajustata ma sama pathha kinchana
govindeti harer nama geyam gayasva nityasah

(Skanda Purana)

-

Do not recite the Rig, Yajur, Sama or Atharva Veda. Just chant the holy name of Lord 'Govinda' incessantly.

#11 The Holy name of Krishna is superior to the holy names of 'Vishnu' and 'Rama'

Sri Chaitanya Mahaprabhu had explained :

<u>Every Name of Lord Vishnu</u> is superior to all the Vedas. Know that the name 'Rama' is superior to a thousand names of Lord Vishnu.

*vishnor ekaika-namapi
sarva-vedadhikam matam
Tadrk-nama-sahasrena
'Rama'-nama-samamsmrtam*

(Padma Purana)

-

Every single name of 'Vishnu' is superior to all the Vedas. The Name 'Rama' is superior to a thousand names of Vishnu.

The results achieved by chanting a thousand names of 'Vishnu' three times is the same that is attained by chanting the Holy Name of Krishna just once.

*sahasra-namnam punyanam triravrttya tu yat phalam
ekavrttya tu krsnasya namaikam tat prayachchhati*

(Brahmanda Purana)

Website - www.thegaudiyatreasuresofbengal.com

The result which is achieved by chanting a thousand names of 'Vishnu' three times is the same that is attained by chanting the Holy Name of Krishna just once.

"*Krishna Krishna Krishna Krishna Krishna Krishna Krishna he!*" .O devotees! Incessantly chant this Holy name (Hare Krishna Mahamantra).

*'Hare Krishna Hare Krishna Krishna Krishna Hare Hare
Hare Rama Hare Rama Rama Rama Hare Hare'*

Chanting these sixteen Holy Names ensures that all spiritual obligations are satisfied. One who chants them is bestowed with all perfections in spiritual life. The benefits of chanting the Hare Krishna Mahamantra are unlimited.

*SRI SRI RADHA PRANAVALLAV JIU,
WORSHIPABLE DEITY OF KANAI THAKURA*

#12 Chanting of the Holy Name of Lord Hari is superior to any pilgrimage

*kuruksetrena kim tasya kim kasya puskarena va
jihvagre vasati yasya harir ity aksara-dvayam
(Skanda purana)*

-

What is the need of touring Kurukshetra, Kashi or Pushkara for one whose tongue is always blessed with the two syllables 'Ha-ri'?

*tirtha-koti-sahasrani tirtha-koti-satani ca
tani sarvany avapnoti vishnor namanukirtanat*

(Vamana Purana)

-

What one cannot obtain after touring millions and billions of holy places is achieved simply by chanting the holy names of Lord Vishnu.

Sitting at Kurukshetra, Visvamitra Muni once said, 'I have heard the names of various holy places of pilgrimage in this world. But none of them are even one-millionth as potent as chanting the Holy Name of Lord Hari'. This statement is of utmost value.

*visrutani bahunyeva tirthani bahudhani ca
koty amsena na tulyani nama-kirtanato hareh*

(Visvamitra Samhita)

-

None of the renowned holy places of this world are even one-millionth as potent as chanting the Holy Name of Lord Hari.

*kintata vedagama sastra-vistarais
tirthair anekair api kim prayojanam*

yady atmano vanchasi mukti-karanam
govinda govinda iti sphuratam rata

(Laghu Bhagavata)

-

My child, What is the need for studying the voluminous Vedas and its corollaries? And what is the need of so many holy sites of pilgrimage? One who aspires to get delivered from this material world should constantly chant 'Govinda' 'Govinda'.

#13 Chanting the Holy Name is superior to all pious activities

Prayaga-gangodaka-kalpa-vasah
yajnayutam meru-suvarna-danam
govinda-kirterna samam satamsaih
(Laghu Bhagavatah)

-

The actions of donating millions of cows during solar eclipses, staying at sacred Prayag by the Ganges for a Kalpa (billions of years comprising a cycle of the 4 yugas), offering countless sacrifices or donating Mount

Sumeru's worth of Gold in charity does not compare to even one-hundredth the value of chanting the Lord Govinda's Holy Name.

The scriptures state that public welfare works, no matter how numerous or extensive, are after all mundane activities.

The Holy Name of Lord Hari easily grants one liberation from this material world. Fruitive activities are trivial when compared to the Holy Name of the Lord.

istapurtani karmani subahuni kritany api bhava hetuni tany-eva harer nama tu muktidaam

(Baudhayana samhita)

-

Public welfare works, numerous or extensive, are after all mundane activities.The Holy Name of Lord Hari easily grants one liberation from this material world.

#14 Chanting the Holy Name is superior to the practice of Sankhya and Ashtanga Yoga

kim karishyati sankhyena kim yogair nara nayaka
muktim-ichchhasi rajendra kuru govinda-kirtanam

(Garuda Purana)

-

O King, What will you do with Sankhya Yoga (path of deductive philosophical speculation) or Astanga Yoga (eightfold mystic yoga) processes? If you are searching for liberation then incessantly chant the holy name of Govinda.

aho bata svapaco to gariyan
yaj jihvagre vartate nama tubhyam
tepus tapas te juhuvuh sasnur arya
brahmanuchur nama grnanti ye te
(Srimad Bhagavatam, 3.33.7)

-

Oh, how glorious! Even an outcast on whose tongue appears Your holy name is worshipable! Persons who chant the holy name of Your Lordship must have performed severe austerities, fire sacrifices and achieved all the good manners of the Aryans. To chant Your holy name, they must have bathed at holy sites of pilgrimage, studied all the Vedic scriptures and fulfilled everything needed.

#15 Lord Krishna and His holy name is non-different

The Holy Name of the Supreme Lord is all-powerful and is equal to Lord Krishna in all respects. Lord Krishna has invested all of His potencies within His holy name.

Lord Krishna has drawn His powers present within the practice of charity, religious rituals, austerity, visiting holy sites of pilgrimages, Karma-Kanda rituals for the demigods, rajasuya yajna, asvamedha yajna, knowledge of self-

Website - www.thegaudiyatreasuresofbengal.com

realization and has invested them in His Holy Name.

dana-vrata-tapas-tirtha-kshetradinam ca yah sthitah
saktayo deva-mahatam sarva-papah-harah subhah
rajasuyasvamedhanam jnanam adhyatma-vastunah
akrsiya harina sarvah sthapitah svesu namasu

(Skanda Purana)

-

The Lord has drawn all of His purifying power invested within the practice of charity, religious rituals, austerity, visiting holy sites of pilgrimages, Karma-Kanda rituals that are offered unto the demigods, rajasuya yajna, asvamedha yajna, knowledge of self-realization and has infused them into His Names.

How to Chant the Hare Krishna Mahamantra ?

Now that we understand the benefits of chanting the Hare Krishna Mahamantra and its glories, we should learn how to chant the Mantra properly. One should chant in such a manner that the Holy name of Krishna is suitably glorified. The valor of the Holy name **never unveils** itself wherever there is any uncertainty regarding the Holy name's potency. The grace of the holy name of the Supreme Lord Sri Krishna (and the benefits of chanting the Hare Krishna Mahamantra) can only be attained by the faithful and not by the skeptical. This is an esoteric mystery which the devotees should certainly be aware of.

One should chant the following Hare Krishna Mahamantra preferrably on Tulasi beads -

Hare Krishna Hare Krishna Krishna Krishna Hare Hare, Hare Rama Hare Rama Rama Rama Hare Hare

This Hare Krishna Mahamantra also finds its mention in the Kali santarana Upanishad, wherein it has been described as the destroyer of all inauspiciousness *(iti sodasakam namnam kali kalmasa nashanam)*. The Supreme Lord, appearing as Sri Chaitanya Mahaprabhu, has inspired us one and all to incessantly chant the holy name of Krishna. He has further instructed us to make an effort and preach extensively to others ,about the glories of chanting Krishna's holy name (*yare dekho taare kaha Krishna upadesha...*). It is very important that we seek shelter of Sri Chaitanya Mahaprabhu and His associates before we begin chanting each round of the Hare Krishna Mahamantra. So first of all we should chant the below Pancha Tattva Mahamantra before we proceed to chant the Hare Krishna Mahamantra.

'Jaya Sri Krishna Chaitanya, Prabhu Nityananda ,Sri Advaita, Gadadhara, Srivasa adi Gaura bhakta vrinda'

Translation - *I offer my respectful obeisances unto Sri Chaitanya Mahaprabhu, Lord Nityananda, Sri Advaita, Gadadhara Pandit, Srivasa Thakura and all the devotees of Lord Chaitanya.*

Chanting the holy names of Sri Chaitanya Mahaprabhu and His associates bestows upon us their causeless mercy enabling us to chant Krishna's names without committing any offenses.

Website - www.thegaudiyatreasuresofbengal.com

108 japa beads form a round. On each of these beads, we should chant the complete Hare Krishna Mahamantra (Hare Krishna Hare Krishna Krishna Krishna Hare Hare, Hare Rama Hare Rama Rama Rama Hare Hare) before proceeding to the next bead. A minimum of 16 rounds of Hare Krishna Mahamantra daily is recommended for the most beneficial results considering the present day and age. However, one can begin with chanting any number of rounds and then slowly grow his chanting with time. As stated before, we should chant the Pancha Tattva Mantra at least once before beginning each round of the 'Hare Krishna Mahamantra'.

Meaning of Hare Krishna Mahamantra | Glories of the Hare Krishna Mahamantra

The word 'Hare' refers to the Supreme Lord's internal energy or Srimati Radharani and the word 'Krishna' refers to Lord Krishna, the supreme personality of Godhead. When we chant the Hare Krishna Mahamantra, we pray to Srimati Radharani, to engage us in the service of Sri Krishna. Rendering devotional service unto the Supreme Lord is the very essence of our existence and the ultimate perfection of our lives. Also, as Lord Gauranga (Sri Chaitanya Mahaprabhu) is non-different from Sri Radha and Krishna *(Sri Krishna Chaitanya ,Radha Krishna Nahe anya),* the syllables 'Hare Krishna' is non-different from Lord Gauranga. So when we chant the Hare Krishna Mahamantra, we pray to Lord Chaitanya to engage us in His glorious Harinama sankirtana movement.

The Twenty-six Qualities of a devotee

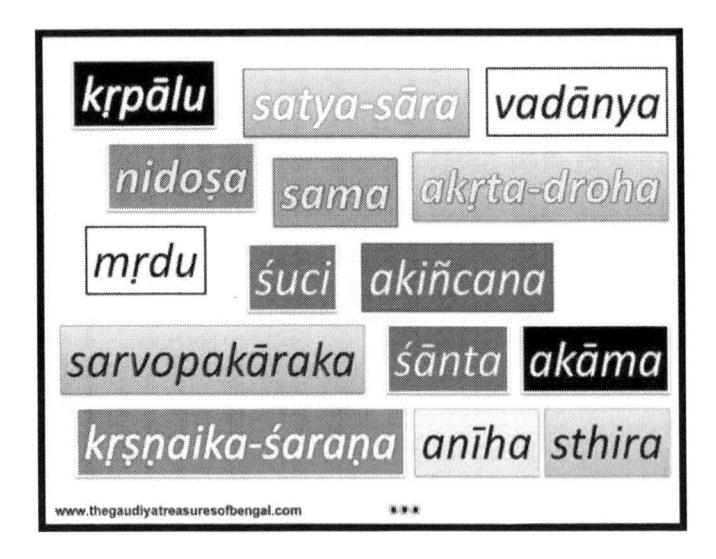

kṛpālu	satya-sāra	vadānya
nidoṣa	sama	akṛta-droha
mṛdu	śuci	akiñcana
sarvopakāraka	śānta	akāma
kṛṣṇaika-śaraṇa	anīha	sthira

Now that we understand the very basics of Bhakti yoga, it is worthwhile for us to invest our time, and realize the magnanimity of an elevated Vaishnava, a pure devotee of the Lord. Reading Sri Chaitanya Caritamrta, we come to understand that out of the innumerable godly qualities, there are twenty-six ,which are very prominent within a devotee of Krishna. Sri Krishnadasa Kaviraja (the author of Chaitanya Charitamrita), out of his causeless mercy, has

Website - www.thegaudiyatreasuresofbengal.com

listed them down (Madhya Lila 22.78-80) for our meditation and contemplation.

sei saba guna haya vaishnava lakshana
saba kaha na yaya, kari dig darashana

(cc, Madhya, 22.77)

A pure devotee is magnanimous and an inspiration to one and all. It is only by great fortune, that one gets to associate with him. In Fact even a moment's association with a pure devotee of the Lord is all purifying and it is only by his causeless mercy that one becomes eligible to engage in the service of the Supreme Lord. In this chapter, we shall try to relish and discuss these glorious super excellent qualities that ornament the devotees of the Lord.

- **Kind (Kripalu), Compassionate (karuna) & works for the welfare of everyone (sarva-upakaraka)**: A Vaishnava (devotee) is always merciful and a well-wishing friend of not only humans, but all living beings. A devotee is always concerned with the suffering condition of the living entities entrapped in material existence. He always tries to devise ways and means to relieve them from their suffering.

When Namacharya Haridas Thakur was asked as to why one should chant the Lord's holy names loudly, he replied that when one chants silently, only he receives the benefit, whereas when one chants loudly, everyone around him, even the animals and plants are benefitted from associating with the Lord's holy names. Again when Haridasa Thakura was being dragged and beaten across the twenty-two market places in Phulia, he kept incessantly praying to the Supreme Lord and begged Him to forgive those demoniac guards who were beating him like animals. Sri Chaitanya Mahaprabhu later revealed during Mahaprakash Lila, that if Haridasa Thakura had not then prayed, the Lord would have severed the heads of those miscreants.

Seeing the most abominable Jagai and Madhai, Lord Nityananda and Haridas Thakur felt great compassion and wanted to deliver them from their sinful existence. They urged those drunkards to take up the chanting of the Lord's holy names.As we all know, Jagai and Madhai didn't take the advice well and attacked Nityananda prabhu by hurling broken pots towards Him. The pot struck Nityananda Prabhu upon His forehead and caused Him to bleed profusely. But this could not stop Nitai from continuing to shower His immense compassion upon these sinful souls. When Mahaprabhu wanted to kill Jagai and Madhai , Nityananda prabhu restrained the Lord from doing so. Jagai and Madhai went on to become great devotees and were delivered due to Nityananda Prabhu's immense mercy.

- **Humble, does not quarrel (akrta-droha) & without false prestige (amani)** - A pure devotees of the Lord (Vaishnava) lives by the instructions given by Sri Chaitanya Mahaprabhu – "*trinad api sunicena, taror api sahishnuna, amanina manadena,* *kirtaniya sada hari"* which means that One should chant the holy names of the Lord in a humble state of mind, thinking oneself lower than the straw in the street and be more tolerant than even a tree.One should be devoid of all sense of false prestige, and be ready to offer all respect unto others.

When the famous Digvijayi scholar Roop Narayan challenged Srila Rupa Goswami wanting to debate the scriptures with him, Sri Rupa didn't want to waste his time arguing with such a mundane scholar. Instead he readily accepted defeat and signed his Vijaya Patra (certificate of victory). Roop Narayan could not grasp Sri Rupa Goswami's exalted status and neither could he understand that he had accepted defeat only out of utter humility. Jiva Goswami, however, was very upset seeing Roop Narayan boast, and he accepted the challenge on Rupa Goswami's behalf. Jiva Goswami subsequently debated and defeated Roop Narayan making him realize the elevated stature of Sri Rupa Gosai. Roop Narayan then surrendered unto the lotus feet of Rupa and Sanatana goswami.

Sri Kashishwar pandita was the personal servant of Sri Chaitanya Mahaprabhu in Jagannatha Puri. After Lord Govinda dev jiu had manifested in Vrindavana, Lord Chaitanya ordered Kashishwar to immediately go to Vrindavana and assist Sri Rupa in serving Sri Govinda dev. This instruction was extremely painful for Sri Kashishwar pandita to execute who preferred to even give up his life than abandon the association of Lord Gaurahari. But please note the greatness of this exalted soul, who was ready to easily give up his life but not defy the orders of his master. His personal likings and desires were the least important when it came to executing the orders of the Lord. Thus keeping a stone upon his heart, this great Vaishnava left for Vrindavana and spent the rest of his life serving the deities of Govinda dev jiu. He took along with him a small deity of Sri Chaitanya Mahaprabhu (which

Mahaprabhu Himself had gifted to him), that subsequently became renowned as Gaura-Govinda. He placed this deity in the same altar and worshipped it along with Sri Radha Govinda Dev.

- **Truthful (satya-sara) & Steady, fixed (sthira)** - No matter how difficult the circumstances, a Vaishnava always finds ways and means to remember and serve his supreme master. His entire existence is geared only to satisfy and provide pleasure unto Sri Guru and Gauranga. Sanatana goswami, inspite of his advanced age, made it a point to circumambulate the Govardhana hill daily (around 23 miles). Though it was very difficult for him to undertake this parikrama physically, yet he did not relent. Feeling compassionate, the Supreme Lord gave him His darsana and gifted to him a small Govardhan sila (sacred stone) with His lotus footprint engraved upon it. On request of the Lord, Srila Sanatana used to circumambulate this Govardhan Sila from then on. The

Lord assured him that circumambulating this sacred stone was equivalent to doing Govardhan Parikrama.

We can cite the example of namacharya Haridasa Thakura, who inspite of being very old and physically unwell, continued to chant three lakh holy names of the lord daily. Srila Haridasa did not want to reduce the stipulated number of rounds that he chanted under any circumstances.

A.C Bhaktivedanta Swami Prabhupada, the founder acharya of Iskcon, inspite of failing for forty years of his life ,did not lose hope. Though he was greatly criticized by his own family members for having a spiritual interest, he did not give up his intense desire to serve the mission of his spiritual master. In the process he had to abandon his wife and children, live without proper facilities, travel alone to the west on a cargo ship in which he suffered from heart attacks (he was then 70 years old),etc. As a result of his sacrifice, millions across the world today

Website - www.thegaudiyatreasuresofbengal.com

have the opportunity to lead a Krishna conscious life.

Our Gurudeva, HH Jayapataka Swami Maharaj, has been rendered physically handicapped since he suffered from a stroke in the year 2008. Yet, his advanced age and the difficult physical condition he is in, has not stopped him from preaching all over the world. Travelling on a wheelchair, he continues to provide hope and inspiration to millions.

We should try to learn from these examples and imbibe in our lives the teachings & the service attitude of these great souls.

- **Equal to everyone (sama)** - A vaishnava sees the same supersoul in everyone's heart. Hence he treats whomsoever he meets, whether he be of any caste or creed, any language, culture or background as equal. Lord Chaitanya had taught us *'kiba vipra kiba nyasi sudra kene naya, yei krishna-tattva-vetta, sei guru haya'*. In other words, anyone who is well conversant with the science of Krishna consciousness is eligible to become a Guru, irrespective of whether he is a brahmana, sannyasi or even shudra. There is no consideration of one's background in Chaitanya Mahaprabhu' movement.

We see how Nityananda Prabhu flooded the streets of Bengal with harinama Sankirtana (*'Premer bonya loiya Nitai, aila Gauda deshe, dubilo bhakta jana, dina hina bhashe'*). The waves of ecstasy washed one and all, irrespective of one's qualification or stature. Nityananda Prabhu delivered the gold mercantile community of Saptagram, who were considered fallen during those days.In fact Sri Uddharana datta Thakura, a prominent member of this community, became Nityananda prabhu's personal cook.

Elsewhere we learn how Sri Kalidasa Roy recognized Sri Jharu Thakura to be an exalted devotee, though he was just a sweeper. Sri kalidasa Roy went out of his way and devised ways and means to obtain the prasada remnants of Jharu Thakura.

When Sri Chaitanya Mahaprabhu met Sri Ramananda Raya, he was overwhelmed with ecstatic feelings. Sri Ramananda belonged to a low caste while Mahaprabhu was a sannyasi. Mahaprabhu didn't judge Ramananada on account of his background but on account of his devotion.

When Syamananda pandita (Dukhi Krishna Das) met his spiritual master, Sri Hridaya Chaitanya didn't reject him though Syamananda prabhu belonged to the lowly sadgopa caste. Instead he was overjoyed to accept a sincere and dedicated disciple as Syamananda pandita.

- **Faultless (nidosa)** - A Vaishnava, who in words, deeds, and mind is completely surrendered unto Krishna and executes Guru and Krishna's desire to the best of his ability is always faultless.

Website - www.thegaudiyatreasuresofbengal.com

Sri Ramananda Raya, although he used to personally dress the Devadasis and teach the young girls how to physically express all the moods of love before Jagannath Deva, has been greatly glorified by Sri Chaitanya Mahaprabhu. Sri Ramananda Raya was a maha bhagavata (great devotee), an eternal associate of the Lord, who possessed no desire for personal sense gratification. Though he had to touch these girls in order to teach them, yet his mind was not disturbed in the slightest. His consciousness was forever rooted unto the lotus feet of the Lord.

- **Magnanimous (vadanya) , mild (mrdu), Peaceful (santa) & without material possessions (akincana)** - Sri Nityananda Prabhu, who is none other than the incarnation of Lord Balarama, used to beg from door to door, urging people to chant the holy name of Lord Gauranga *(Amare Kiniya laho bhojo Gaurahari)*. Holding straws between His teeth, rolling on the dusty grounds, He requested them again and again to chant. The Lord did not mind to play the role of a beggar just to deliver His children from their material existence. Such is the magnanimity of Nityananda prabhu. He didn't mind getting beaten by drunkards like Jagai and Madhai, because delivering the sinful was more important than His own personal comforts.

We see the example of Gadadhara Das who delivered the sinful Kazi by making him chant the names of Lord Hari. He took a risk in approaching Kazi, who was feared by everyone. But a vaishnava doesn't think twice, in taking risks for preaching the glories of the Lord.

A devotee is always peaceful, satisfied and doesn't hanker for material possessions. When Sri Chaitanya came to Bengal to visit Saci mata, He stopped over for a few days at Srivasa pandita's house at Kumarhatta (Halisahar). Mahaprabhu was then amazed to notice that Srivasa Pandita did not go out to earn but instead just sat and chanted in his house for the whole day.When Mahaprabhu asked Srivasa pandita as to how he maintained his family, Srivasa replied that by Mahaprabhu's mercy he and his family members never suffer from any shortage. Srivasa pandita added that if ever in future the situation arose that there was no food in the house, then he would wait for three days.If even after three days the situation did not improve then he would commit suicide by jumping into the Ganges. Lord Chaitanya then reassured Srivasa pandita that such a day would never arrive. The Lord then assured that for His devotees, He Himself bore all responsibility of their maintenance. The Lord also quoted a verse from Bhagavad Gita to support His statement, wherein He had stated that for His dear devotees, He personally preserved what they have and carry what they lack (*ananyas chintayanto mam ye janah paryupasate, tesam nityabhiyuktanaam yoga ksemam vahamy aham*). A Vaishnava hence always keeps his faith upon the Lord's protection *(abashya rakshibe krishna - visvasa palana).*

Kolavecha Sridhar was a banana leaf seller of Navadvipa. He was a materially impoverished person who could barely make his ends meet. Yet he was a great devotee of the Lord. Inspite of his financial predicament,whatever little he earned,he used to spend fifty percent of it in worshipping mother Ganges. Mahaprabhu, when He was a little boy, used to go the markets and bargain with him everyday. Finally the Lord used to take away the banana leaves from Sridhar without paying any money.Chaitanya Mahaprabhu loved him a lot. During the Mahaprakash Lila, the Lord was ready to grant Sridhar any boon - the kingdom of Indra, or even the elusive perfections of the mystic yogic process. But Sridhar did not ask for any money or opulence as a benediction; all he wanted was to serve Sri Chaitanya Mahaprabhu life after life.

'Lord, if You must give me something,

then I ask for this. May that Brahmin who used to pinch my banana leaves and bark everyday ,be my Lord, lifetime after lifetime. May that Brahmin who used to argue with me be my master, and I serve His lotus feet.' (Chaitanya Bhagavat 2.9.223-5)

The beautiful pastimes of Kolavecha Sridhar indicate how the devotees of the lord are simple without any material hankerings.

- **Cleanliness (Suci) , Desireless (akama), Self-Controlled (Free from lust, anger, greed, illusion, madness and envy)** - Cleanliness not only refers to that of one's body, but also that of one's mind and consciousness. The Vaishnava etiquettes, like getting up in the morning, washing feet after eating,taking bath after visiting the bathroom for clearing,etc not only keeps one's body clean, but also helps clean one's consciousness. These Vaishnava etiquettes along with strictly following

the regulative principles like no meat eating, no intoxication, no gambling and abstaining from illicit sex, helps one to be established in the mode of pure goodness. When one reaches such a state of consciousness, it is very easy for him to completely surrender unto the lotus feet of the Lord. By the mercy of the lord, such a person no longer possesses any material desires and is delivered from the clutches of lust, greed,anger,illusion,madness ,envy, etc
If we study the recent history, we shall realize how the lives of the hippies, who once led exceedingly unclean and impure lives, have been completely transformed after taking up the process of Krishna consciousness. Strictly following the Vaishnava etiquettes, and the regulative principles, they have been delivered from their material hankerings and have become leaders of the society today. In Fact several of them have become spiritual leaders who provide inspiration and guidance to millions. Being free from lust,greed, anger, illusion,madness and envy, they have dedicated their lives

in the service of the Lord and humanity.

- **Exclusively surrendered to Krishna (Krishnaika Sarana)** - A Vaishnava depends on Krishna in all circumstances. He never thinks of himself to be the doer but considers himself to be an insignificant tool through whom the Lord manifests His own desires. In this regard, we can cite the awe inspiring pastime of Sri Gopal Singh, the king of Bishnupur.The 55th Malla king,Sri Gopal Singh was extremely pious and devoted to the lord. Day and night he immersed himself in singing and chanting the glories of his ishta deva,Sri Madana Mohana.Drawn to its wealth and prosperity, fifty-two thousand Maratha soldiers once attacked the town of Bishnupur. These Marathas were referred to as 'Bargi' in common dialect and were known to be exceedingly ferocious who did not spare even women and children to achieve their ends. They looted wealth, killed people, and before departing, burnt down entire villages. So when these Marathas surrounded Bishnupur, the citizens naturally got very nervous. But King Gopal singh, instead of preparing to retaliate, decided to take complete shelter of his beloved Madana Mohana. He led a tumultuous Harinama sankirtana party that traversed the entire city and filled its land and sky with the auspicious vibrations of the holy name. He asked his soldiers to seek shelter of the Lord and pray for protection.Not all were convinced with his actions though. Towards the end of the night, frightening sounds of cannons were heard. These cannons destroyed the entire army of these marathas and the dreaded Bargi leader almost died in the fight. Suffering a heavy defeat, the 'Bargis' retreated.The next morning, while victory was being celebrated, the king enquired of the brave fighter.The soldiers denied to have fired the cannon and confessed that it was humanly impossible to fire so many shots from these few cannons ,in such a quick succession.

One of the soldiers, then recounted a hair

raising incident. He recollected that while he was guarding the forts the previous night, he saw a young boy, wearing a blue apparel, come out of the city, riding on his white horse. The whole atmosphere was surcharged with pleasant fragrance and the effulgence of His body illuminated the surroundings. The guard said that he had fainted on seeing His enchanting beauty. He regained his senses upon hearing the loud shots of the cannon and observed dead and fleeing maratha warriors, all around. But in spite of searching, he could not find the young boy again. While the King was thus conversing with his soldiers, a milkman came rushing. He informed of a young boy, wearing blue garments, who had stopped the milkman on his way and had eaten all the curd that he was bringing for the king. The boy had a bright smile on His face and identified Himself as the King's son. As a proof, the boy had also handed over His bracelet to the milkman, which He had asked to be shown to His father, so that the King could pay him the required money. The milkman added, that the boy had claimed to be very tired fighting the Marathas all night and needed something cool to eat. The boy had marks of explosives all over His beautiful body.

Sri Gopal Singh began shedding tears of joy. He understood who that small boy was. He was none other than his beloved Madana Mohana who had mercifully responded to the prayers of His devotees and had protected them from grave danger. On opening the temple gates, Sri Madanamohana was found standing, with His blue garments completely drenched in perspiration. The marks of explosives as if decorated His enchanting form and His bracelet was missing from His right hand. Being entranced, the King fainted in ecstasy. We humbly beg at the feet of Sri Gopal singh to bestow upon us a tiny drop from the ocean of unflinching faith he possesses for the Supreme Lord.

Website - www.thegaudiyatreasuresofbengal.com

- **Indifferent to material acquisitions (aniha), without inebriation (apramatta) & without false prestige (amani)** - Sri Pundarika Vidyanidhi was a great branch of Lord Chaitanya's desire tree of devotional service. He was so dear to the Lord that the Lord would sometimes cry in his absence (...*yanra nama lana prabhu kandila apani*). Pundarika hailed from a village known as Mekhala, situated in the Chattagram district of Bangladesh.He was a zamindar(landlord) and he disguised his external appearance as a wealthy materialist. In fact his external appearance was so deceiving with all the rich paraphernalia he possessed, that even Gadadhara Pandita mistook him to be an ordinary wealthy person devoid of Vaishnava qualities. When the two met, Pundarika, was comfortably seated upon a soft mattress supporting his back with silk pillows.Above his head were three tiers of ornamented canopies and there were large mirrors on his either side into which he frequently glanced. Pundarika's hair was well groomed and they looked shiny with perfumed oil. Behind him were two men fanning him with peacock feathers. Observing the opulence that surrounded Pundarika, Sri Gadadhara Pandita, who was very renounced from His very childhood, could not grasp his elevated stature and mistook him to be an ordinary materialist.

Mukunda Datta, who was also present over there, could understand Gadadhara's mind and took it upon himself to reveal the real nature of Pundarika. With his sweet voice, he began reciting a verse describing the glories of Sri Krishna. He asked as to how one can be more merciful than He, who had granted the position of mother to the she-demon Putana, who wanted to kill Him by smearing poison on her breast. Just by offering her breast and by wanting to feed little Krishna, even though her actual desire was to poison Him, the demon Putana had achieved liberation and the exalted status of His mother. As soon as Sri Pundarika heard

Website - www.thegaudiyatreasuresofbengal.com

this verse, he became absorbed in an intense spiritual emotion and rolled over the ground in ecstasy.He smashed all the valuable paraphernalia that surrounded him,and began tearing off his costly clothes.Incessantly shedding tears ,he cried out for the association of the Supreme Lord. The storm of ecstatic love abated when Sri Pundarika fell down unconscious, remaining submerged in an ocean of bliss. Seeing the transcendental symptoms of love on Pundarika's body, Gadadhara pandit realized his mistake and began to repent. Even though Pundarika Vidyanidhi was a great Vaishnava, he kept it a secret and appeared just like a materialistic person. Gadadhara Pandita ultimately took initiation from Pundarika Vidyanidhi to atone for his offenses.Thus we understand the exalted position of Pundarika Vidyanidhi who though being a very rich landlord, was indifferent towards his material possessions when it came to exhibiting his love for the lord. For such an elevated soul, it does not matter whether he lives in the house or in the forest, whether he wears a loincloth or wears the garb of a king. Pundarika was indifferent towards his material possessions and put on the show of being sensualist for those who were capable of being deceived by someone's external appearance. The lotus feet of Pundarika Vidyanidhi are the worshipable treasure-house of the devotees.

Similarly, Mukunda Das, who served as the King's physician in Malda (Gauda), was a great Vaishnava devotee. Sri Chaitanya Mahaprabhu greatly glorified Sri Mukunda's devotion towards the Lord and compared it to pure gold (...*nigooda nirmala prema, yena dagdha hema*). Externally Sri Mukunda acted as a physician and served the king, but internally he was a pure devotee whose depths of love (for the lord) was very difficult to ascertain. One day while Mukunda and the erstwhile king, Nawab Hussain Shah, were discussing medical science, one of the king's servants arrived and started fanning the king with a fan made of peacock feathers. He held the fan above the king's head. Just by seeing the peacock feathers, Sri Mukunda became absorbed in the pastimes of his beloved Krishna and began meditating upon Sri Vrindavana dham. Contemplating thus, he fell down from the high sitting platform onto the ground. When Sri Mukunda came back to his senses, the king inquired as to what had happened to him. In order not to reveal his ecstatic mood, Mukunda then lied that he had been suffering from a disease like epilepsy, due to which he often falls unconscious. But the king, being very intelligent, understood the whole affair and realized that Sri Mukunda was a great liberated personality.

Thus we understand that the external appearance of a person can be very deceiving. A devotee, no matter where he resides or what profession he is engaged in, is completely surrendered and continuously mediates upon the Supreme Lord. He is neither overwhelmed by the riches he possesses nor does he harbour any false prestige. He only identifies himself as the servant of the servant of the Supreme Lord (Dasanudas).

- **Does not eat more than required (mita-bhuk)** - A devotee of the Lord does not eat too much or too little. He lives moderately and does not eat more than required to maintain his body. If we consider the examples of the six goswamis of Vrindavan, we find that they lived by doing madhukari (collected food by begging from door to door). In this way they purified those from whom they begged, by accepting their charity. We can also cite the example of Shuklambar brahmacari, who kept his body and soul together by offering and eating the foodstuffs that he daily accumulated by begging. Since he was constantly absorbed in the joys of chanting the names of the Lord and remembering His qualities and pastimes, he never suffered from any poverty. Though to an ordinary conditioned soul he appeared to be a poverty-stricken mendicant, but to the transcendental eyes ,he was very rich because of his intense love for Mahaprabhu. Lord Chaitanya out of His causeless mercy and love for Shuklambar used to snatch the dry rice from his bag and eat it. Though Shuklambar was pained to see the Lord eat the unclean and broken fragments of low-quality rice and felt that he was committing an offense,the Lord calmed him and assured him that He always enjoyed eating His Devotee's food with great enthusiasm.On the other hand the Lord had no interest whatsoever in eating the finest foodstuffs belonging to a non devotee.

- **Expert (daksha)** - A pure devotee of the Lord is empowered by the Lord and the spiritual master to perform great feats. When the books of the Goswamis were stolen in Bishnupur, Srinivasa Acharya did not lose his cool. Instead he meditated and sought inspiration. Ultimately he managed to not only recover the books but also initiated the culprit King Bir Hambir, who went on to become a great Vaishnava himself.

Similarly, A.C Bhaktivedanta Swami Prabhupada, the founder acharya of Iskcon, has accomplished feats which are difficult for one to even try and imagine. At the advanced age of seventy, boarding a cargo ship, without any money, he travelled alone to the United States. He suffered from two heart attacks during this journey. In the next ten years, he established this world wide Krishna consciousness movement, encircled the globe fourteen times and opened 108 Hare krishna temples across six continents. By the time he passed away in 1977, he had initiated more than 5000 disciples and launched the ISKCON life membership program enrolling thousands of members.

- **Grave (gambhira), Friend (maitra), Silent (Mauni) & Poet (Kavi)** - A Vaishnava is always relishing the transcendental mellows of the pastimes of Sri Radha and Krishna. He is always contemplating upon the glories of the Lord. He knows that the material world is temporary and that the material existence can come to an abrupt end at any point of time.So a devotee is never overwhelmed or carried away and is always focused on his eternal journey back home, back to godhead. Hence a devotee is always grave, silent and serious about his spiritual life.

At the same time, he tries to help the living entities by giving them the supreme Knowledge and encouraging them to practice spirituality.So naturally, he is the best friend that one can possibly have.

A Vaishnava also develops poetic qualities, that enables him to compose poems glorifying the Lord and His devotees.The Mahabharata written by Srila Vyasadeva is the longest poem in the world.The Mahabharata is roughly ten times the length of the Iliad and the Odyssey combined. When a devotee wishes to glorify the Lord or His pastimes, he invariably takes the refuge of poems, wherein he can express his feelings in an apt manner. The Gaudiya Vaishnava bhajans(songs) written by [Narottama Das Thakura](), Locana Das Thakur, Vrindavan Das Thakur, Bhaktivinoda Thakura and other prominent vaishnavas help us relish their feelings and depths of devotion and inspire us follow in their footsteps.

Biographies of Sri Chaitanya Mahaprabhu namely Sri Chaitanya Caritamrta, Chaitanya Bhagavata and Chaitanya Mangala are the greatest bengali classics to have been ever written.

Devotee of Lord Krishna | Power of devotee association

Sri Rupa Goswami, foremost of the six Goswamis of Vrindavana, delineates the actions that help boost one's devotional life and those that serve as impediments hindering one's spiritual progress. He writes in his 'Nectar of Instructions' that associating with worldly-minded people, who are not drawn to devotion, is one such action that is detrimental to spiritual progress *(jana sangas ca laulyam ca sadbhir bhaktir vinashyati)*. He therefore urges a serious devotee of Lord Krishna to renounce such material association in order to achieve success in his/her spiritual endeavors *(sanga tyagat sato vritteh sadbhir bhaktih prasidhyati)*. The Vedic Literatures are full of such evidences that establish the sublime benefits of associating with a pure devotee of the Supreme Lord (Sri Krishna). Spirituality fosters in the association of devotees while materialistic company promotes materialistic pursuits. Hence the wise choose their association carefully acknowledging that their consciousness is affected by the company they keep.

Spirit and matter are fundamentally opposed to each other. One can either live in spiritual or else in material consciousness. Likewise, material and spiritual attachments are inversely proportional to each other. Lord Krishna, the Supreme Lord, is the master of countless potencies.

parasya saktir vividhaiva sruyate - His energies are innumerable and immeasurable (Svetasvatara Upanishad 6.8)

These potencies can be grouped primarily into internal, marginal, and external. The internal energy of the Supreme Lord constitutes the eternal, blissful, and cognizant spiritual world.

Those who possess a spiritual consciousness and seek the shelter of the Supreme Lord fall within the purview of the Lord's internal energy (Hladini shakti). On the other hand, this temporary world of matter falls within the purview of the Lord's external energy (Bahiranga shakti). The living entities of this world, however, belong to a third category. They belong to the marginal potency or the 'tatastha shakti' of the Supreme Lord. 'Tata' refers to the region between land and water, and hence it holds the properties of both. Therefore 'tata' cannot be referred to as belonging purely to either land or water. Similarly, the living entities of this world have a choice to be attracted to either the world of spirit or the world of matter. Though the living entity is a part and parcel of the Supreme Lord and spiritual by nature, yet sometimes it may become overwhelmed by this temporary world of dull matter. Those living beings who grow bewildered by the illusory energy (Maya) of the Lord and consequently try to enjoy this temporary material world, become controlled by the external potency (bahiranga shakti) of the Supreme Lord. These unfortunate souls deviate from their constitutional position as a servant of the Supreme Lord and indulge in sense gratification by trying to Lord over matter. However, their efforts only die in frustration as flickering sensual pleasures can never fully satisfy a living being who is eternally hankering for pure spiritual bliss. On the other hand, those wise living entities (devotee of Krishna), who choose to engage in the devotional service of the Supreme Lord become controlled by the Lord's internal energy (Hladini shakti).

In the absence of the association of pure devotees, it becomes exceedingly hard for a living entity to escape the external energy of the Supreme Lord. The Bhagavad Gita teaches how this material energy of the Lord is exceedingly difficult for a living being to overcome on his own *(mama maya duratyaya)*. But this incredibly challenging objective is easily accomplished by those who surrender unto the Supreme Lord and seek His divine shelter *(mam eva ye prapadyante mayam etam taranti te)*. Such a fortunate soul is rare in these three worlds. The association of devotees assumes great significance in this regard as it reminds a living entity of the grave misfortunes of leading a materialistic life and helps him pursue the ultimate objective of engaging in devotional service of the Supreme Lord. That is why even the great Vaishnava poet Narottama das Thakura hankers for the association of devotees and sings - *'grihe ba vanete thake, ha Gauranga bole dake, Narottama mange tara sanga' (Narottama das seeks the association of one who calls out the name of 'Gauranga' with love. It does not matter if such a person stays in his house or being renounced, stays in the forest).*

Pastimes from various revealed scriptures that exhibit the importance of associating with a devotee of the Supreme Lord (Sri Krishna) and avoiding the association of Non-devotees

A devotee named **Kala Krishna das** accompanied Sri Chaitanya Mahaprabhu on His tour of South India *(Chaitanya Charitamrita, Madhya, Ch 9)*. But unfortunately, he deviated from Mahaprabhu's personal service being allured by the Bhattatharis (gypsies) who were then living in the region of Mallara-Desha (the area around northern Kerala and southern Karnataka). Bhattatharis are a nomadic community who pose as sannyasis but whose real business is stealing and cheating. The Bhattatharis take the help of their women to entice others to cheat them. Kala Krishna das associated with these nomadic people and fell into their trap. On being requested to return Kala Krishna das, the Bhattatharis attacked **Lord Chaitanya** with their weapons. However, owing to Mahaprabhu's divine will, the

Website - www.thegaudiyatreasuresofbengal.com

weapons fell off their hands and struck their own bodies. Finally, Chaitanya Mahaprabhu grabbed Kala Krishna das by his hair and rescued him by pulling him away. Chaitanya Mahaprabhu later rejected Kala Krishna das due to his fall down.

On the other hand, the scriptures are full of pastimes that exhibit the power of devotee association. For instance, **dacoit Ratnakara** was transformed into sage **Valmiki**, coming in association with Narada muni, an exalted devotee of Krishna. Valmiki went on to compose the great epic Ramayana that is replete with enchanting pastimes of Lord Rama and His dear devotees.

In the pastimes of Namacharya Haridasa Thakura *(Chaitanya Charitamrita, Antya, 3.99-144)*, we observe how the **prostitute Lakshahira (Hira bai)** who had come to seduce and defame Haridasa, met with a change of heart. Associating with **Haridasa Thakura**, a pure devotee of Lord Krishna, and hearing him chant the holy names of Krishna for three consecutive days, purified her and raised her consciousness. She acknowledged her crime and later accepted initiation from Thakura Haridasa. She distributed her wealth, shaved off her head, and spent the rest of her life engaging herself in the service of Lord Krishna.

Gangadhara Bhattacharya, the father of Srinivasa acharya, was one of those who had the rare opportunity to witness Sri Chaitanya Mahaprabhu's sannyasa initiation at Gauranga bari ,in Katwa *(ref - Bhakti ratnakara, ch 2)*. It was very heartbreaking for those present, to witness Lord Chaitanya ,whose beauty surpassed that of a millions of moons, shave off His beautiful hairs and accept the robes of a renunciant. At the same time, those present were immersed in a wave of ecstasy, being able to behold the Lord's beautiful form, and His captivating intoxicated mood. Such was the purifying effect of catching a glimpse of Lord Chaitanya and witnessing His sannyasa, that Gangadhara began chanting Sri Chaitanya's names day and night. He constantly cried "Ha Chaitanya! Ha Chaitanya! Krishna Chaitanya!". Such was his intoxication in divine love for Mahaprabhu, that people nicknamed him as **Chaitanya Das**. This is how, being a recipient of Lord Gauranga's mercy, Sri Gangadhara Bhattacharya came to be subsequently known as Chaitanya Das. He and his wife Lakshmipriya devi were blessed by Lord Chaitanya, and as a result these fortunate souls could subsequently become the proud parents of Sri Srinivasa Acharya, the manifestation of Chaitanya Mahaprabhu's ecstasy.

Srimati Narayani devi was showered with special mercy by Lord Chaitanya while she was just a little child. Once while Sri Gaurasundara was manifesting His divine pastimes at Srivasa

Angana, He ordered little Narayani, who was then just four years old, to chant the holy name of Lord Krishna and cry in ecstasy. Receiving the Lord's mercy and His divine association, little Narayani immediately chanted the holy names and fainted onto the ground, being overwhelmed with ecstatic emotions. Tears of love streamed down her eyes, and flooded the ground. Sri Chaitanya Mahaprabhu was the supreme Lord (Krishna) Himself who had advented in the mood of a devotee of Krishna. This pastime with Narayani devi has been very nicely captured by <u>Srila Vrindavana Das</u> in Chaitanya Bhagavata -

Sarva-Bhuta antaryami Sri Gauranga Chand
Agnya kaila 'Narayani Krishna bali kand'
Chari batsarer sei unmatta carita
'Ha Krishna' baliya matra parila bhumita
Anga bahi pare dhara prithibira tale
Paripurna haila sthala nayaner jale

(Sri Chaitanya Bhagavata)

Narayani devi later gave birth to Srila Vrindavana das Thakura, the original Vyasadeva of Lord Chaitanya's pastimes. Srila Vrindavana das is the composer of Chaitanya Bhagavata, the enchanting biography of Sri Chaitanya Mahaprabhu.

Sri Chaitanya Mahaprabhu has set a precedent on how one should be exceedingly eager to associate with devotees. At the same time, one should carefully avoid the association of non-devotees. Chaitanya Mahaprabhu used to engage in ecstatic sankirtana with devotees every night at the house of Srivasa Pandita. Sri Advaita, Haridasa, Srivasa, Mukunda Datta, Gadadhara, and several other devotees accompanied the Lord in these divine pastimes. All of these pastimes took place behind closed doors denying the smartas (ritualistic brahmanas) and the atheists of Nabadwip the opportunity to witness them. These materialists, however, gathered outside the gate and spent their time criticizing the Lord and His sankirtana. But no matter how hard they tried, and how much chaos they created, **Sri**

Chaitanya was exceedingly careful in not allowing them to associate with the devotees or His intimate pastimes. In one such instance, **Srivasa Pandita** even dragged his **mother-in-law** out of the house when she was found hiding at a corner hoping to witness Mahaprabhu's ecstatic dance.

Likewise, during the Mahaprakash Lila (sath prahariya Lila), Sri Chaitanya Mahaprabhu initially refused to bestow His mercy upon **Mukunda Datta** as he was prone to associating with the Mayavadis (Advaita Vedantists). In this way, Chaitanya Mahaprabhu stressed the importance of associating with devotees and at the same time taught us how associating with

Website - www.thegaudiyatreasuresofbengal.com

non-devotees can serve as an impediment in our devotional lives.

Associating with pure devotees of Lord Krishna is emphasized throughout the revealed scriptures. In the Madhya Lila of Chaitanya Charitamrita, it is proclaimed that even a moment's association with a pure devotee of the Lord bestows all success.

> *sadhu-sanga, sadhu-sanga sarva sashtre kaya*
> *lava-matra sadhu-sange sarva-siddhi haya*
> *(Chaitanya Charitamrita, Madhya, 22.54)*

Receiving the association of devotees is an outcome of causeless mercy

Srila Narottama das Thakura sings :

> *ara kabe Nitai-cander koruna hoibe*
> *samsara-basana mora kabe tuccha ha'be*
> *visaya chariya kabe suddha habe*

mana
kabe hama herabo sri-vrindavana

-

When will I obtain the mercy of moon-like Lord Nityananda? When will the fire of my material desires get extinguished?

When will my mind become free from material desires and anxieties? I shall then be able to behold the spiritual abode of Vrindavana

It must be noted that without receiving the mercy of the Lord or the spiritual master, one cannot grow in his/her spiritual life or come into the association of devotees. This principle is highlighted in the above prayer by Narottama das Thakura as well. In this song, he prays to Lord Nityananda, the original Guru, for relieving him of his material entanglement and empowering him to behold the highest spiritual realities.

Sri Raghunath das Goswami, the prayojana acharya of our sampradaya, was the son of a landlord. He tried to leave his home on several occasions. He was driven by an intense desire to associate with the devotees and serve with them full-time. However, his attempts to escape the clutches of his family met with frustration on all occasions. This was until he was blessed by Lord Nityananda and His associates at Panihati. Raghunath's desires came to be fulfilled and he soon obtained the lotus feet of Lord Chaitanya and the association of devotees at Jagannath Puri.

Similarly, Srila Krishnadas Kaviraja Goswami, the composer of Chaitanya Charitamrita, could obtain the shelter of the six

Website - www.thegaudiyatreasuresofbengal.com

Goswamis and the great fortune of residing at Vrindavana dham, only after receiving the causeless mercy of Lord Nityananda *(Chaitanya Charitamrita, Adi, 5.181)*.

Therefore the mercy of the spiritual master is the secret to sustaining our spiritual lives and staying in the association of devotees. His causeless mercy is our only hope in crossing over this vast ocean of material suffering and eventually obtaining the lotus feet of Krishna *(jahara prasade bhai e bhava toriya jai, krishna-prapti hoy jaha hoite)*.

Chaitanya Mahaprabhu - Biography, Teachings & the Hare Krishna Movement

Website - www.thegaudiyatreasuresofbengal.com

Sri Chaitanya Mahaprabhu, the Supreme Personality of Godhead, had mercifully appeared at Yogpeeth (in Mayapur, West Bengal, India) about 500 years ago (in the year 1486 AD), to bless us with the most amazing, profound, and ecstatic pastimes of Gaura Lila. Lord Chaitanya is also called upon by His innumerable names like Gaura, Gauranga, Gaurahari, Nimai, Gaurasundara, etc. In this article, we shall summarize the life, teachings, and biography of Sri Chaitanya Mahaprabhu in a nutshell.

Eminent brahmana, Sri Jagannatha Misra and Saci devi were the proud parents of Lord Chaitanya. The identity of Lord Chaitanya as the Supreme Personality of Godhead can be verified in a number of Vedic scriptures like Srimad Bhagavatam, Mahabharata, Garuda Purana, Nrsimha Purana, Padma purana, Bhavishya Purana, Narada Purana etc. We are quoting just two of such references below, for the pleasure of the devotees.

aham purno bhavisyami yuga sandhyau visesatah

*mayapure navadvipe bhavisyami
saci sutah*

(Garuda Purana)

-

Translation - In the future, in first part of Kali yuga, I shall appear in my complete spiritual form at Mayapura, Navadvipa and become the son of Saci.

The mission of the Lord, along with a description of His golden complexion and how He descends along with His confidential associates in this age of Kali, to inaugurate the Sankirtana Yajna is revealed in Srimad Bhagavatam (Bhagavata purana) -

*Krishna varnam tvishakrishnam
sangopangastra-parsadam
yajnaih sankirtana prayair yajanti
hi sumedhasah*

(Srimad Bhagavatam 11.5.32)

Lord Chaitanya's life and teachings have been instrumental in uniting people across different nationalities, across different backgrounds - be it social, economic, linguistic, cultural. His teachings have been an example of such unity that the United Nations would be very proud of. Sri Chaitanya's teachings have inspired men and women all across the world, to be united in this common cause, to forget their external differences and help each other out in their journey of life - a journey which is as important to the rich as it is to the poor, which is as important to an American as it is to an Indian; a journey which is as important to a Chinese as it is to a Australian. It is not too uncommon these days to hear the chants of 'Hare Krishna' 'Hare Krishna' in the streets of London, Paris, Tokyo or New Delhi. Congregational chanting of 'Hare Krishna', finds its roots in the teachings of Sri Chaitanya Mahaprabhu. Eminent personalities have concluded that Sri Chaitanya's life & teachings have no parallel in human history. Sri Chaitanya's pastimes defy the investigative and the descriptive abilities of phenomenologists and psychologists of religious experience.

Website - www.thegaudiyatreasuresofbengal.com

Sri Chaitanya Mahaprabhu - External reasons for His advent:

Lord Chaitanya though, except for a few rare occasions, had never revealed His identity as the Supreme Lord. He forever remained absorbed in the mood of a devotee. There were several reasons for Lord Chaitanya to appear in this world which have been revealed in detail by Srila Krishnadas Kaviraj Goswami in his nectarian composition, Sri Chaitanya Caritamrta. He writes that Sri Krishna after enacting the sweet pastimes of Vrindavana, pondered over how He had not bestowed the science of unalloyed devotion unto the Supreme, for a long long time. The entire world worships Him in a mood of reverence, strictly following the rules and regulations ordained in the scriptures. However such a worship does not please Him very much, as spontaneous loving attachment, which is the very essence of a relationship, is absent in such a worship.

Aishwarya jnanete saba jagat misrita
Aishwarya sithila preme nahi mora prita
(Chaitanya Caritamrta, adi -3.16)

Website - www.thegaudiyatreasuresofbengal.com

The general populace is very much aware of the six absolute opulences of the Supreme Lord (strength, beauty,wealth, knowledge, fame, renunciation) and hence they visualize and worship the Lord reverentially in His opulent form.Though one who worships this opulent form of the Lord achieves liberation and a destination in the Vaikuntha planets (spiritual world), yet such a person, is largely ignorant of the ecstatic sweet mellows as experienced by the elevated devotees of Vrindavana. The devotees of Vrindavana are always immersed in a mood of spontaneous loving relationship with the Supreme.The Lord now wanted to freely bestow this Supreme benediction of unalloyed devotional service, the highest ecstasy of spirituality, the treasure of the residents of Vrajabhumi (Vrindavan) ,to one and all. He wanted to distribute this Supreme science of Krishna consciousness, receiving which nothing else remains to be achieved, to all the fallen souls of this age of Kali, irrespective of their caste,creed or qualification. Encapturing this deep mood and mission of the Lord ,Srila Bhaktivinoda Thakura sings -

atyanta durlabha prema karibare dana,
sikhaya sharanagati bhakatera prana

-

To bestow this most rare form of divine love, Sri Chaitanya teaches us to surrender, which is the life of all the devotees.

Lord Chaitanya is hence also referred to as 'Maha vadanyaya' or the most munificent ,as He is the most merciful incarnation of the Supreme.

Website - www.thegaudiyatreasuresofbengal.com

Confidential Reasons for Sri Chaitanya Mahaprabhu's appearance:

Apart from propagating the holy names of the Supreme Lord (Krishna) and the science of unconditional devotional service, there was another confidential reason why Lord Chaitanya had descended in this world. The Supreme Personality of Godhead Sri Krishna possessed an intense desire to relish the supreme transcendental bliss that Srimati Radharani experienced by serving Him. Krishna is the Supreme Enjoyer, however, Srimati Radhika, the Supreme enjoyed, experiences a higher degree of ecstasy by serving Sri Krishna.This is something that bewildered even the Supreme Lord and He wanted to experience this first hand, in order to properly appreciate Radharani's position. He also wanted to understand the transcendental mellow of Himself and how He was a reservoir of all sweetness that drove His devotees crazy.hence taking up the mood (bhava) and the golden bodily complexion (kanti) of Srimati Radharani, Sri Krishna descended as Lord Chaitanya in this holy land of Navadvipa.Navadvipa was perceived and created by Srimati Radharani Herself to provide pleasure to Her worshipable master. Sri Chaitanya's heart was an image of Srimati Radhika's emotions - greatly turbulent with the feelings of union (sambhoga) and separation (vipralambha) with Krishna. Hence, it is stated that there is no difference between Lord Chaitanya and the combination of Sri Krishna and Srimati Radharani (*Sri Krishna Chaitanya ,Radha Krishna Nahe anya*). Sri

Website - www.thegaudiyatreasuresofbengal.com

Bhaktisiddhanta Saraswati Thakura exclaims that Sri Chaitanya is not simply Krishna or simply Radhika. Instead, He is the intense embrace of Sri Radha and Krishna. Such is the intensity of their embrace that the divine couple becomes inseparable and merges into one form. Sri Krishna is then ornamented with the deep mood of Radharani and gets completely covered by Her bodily effulgence.Such is the Supreme position of Sri Chaitanya Mahaprabhu.

One should however not confuse these transcendental emotions with the feelings that we experience in our day to day life in relation to other people or any object.It must be pointed out here, that both union and separation from the Supreme Lord produces different states of ecstasy within a devotee.In fact the ecstasy in the mood of separation from the Supreme, is even higher than that in union.This is exactly opposite to what we experience in relation to the petty things of this material world.These uncontrollable feelings became more and more manifested within Lord Chaitanya as His pastimes progressed.During the later stages of His pastime at Gambhira (where Sri Chaitanya resided in Puri) , He was so greatly obsessed with the madness of separation from Krishna, that He exhibited the highest symptoms of ecstasy.

Sri Bara Gauranga, Nitai and Jagannatha, Gauranga Bari, Katwa

The dire situation of India before Sri Chaitanya

Mahaprabhu had appeared in this world:

Before Sri Chaitanya had appeared in Navadvipa, its residents were largely preoccupied with material pursuits. People were egoistic about their material possessions and lacking in God consciousness. Those who engaged in discussing Bhagavad Gita or Srimad Bhagavatam, did not touch upon its essence of devotional service. The holy names of Krishna were nowhere to be heard in the entire town of Navadvipa. Being absorbed in the illusory potency of the Lord, people remained in forgetfulness of their eternal master. They misused their wealth in extravagant wedding ceremonies of their children.

Dambha kari visya-hari puje kon yana
Puttali karoye keho diya bahu dhana
Dhana nashto kare putra kanyara bibhaya
Eimata jagatera byartha kala yaya

(Chaitanya Bhagavata, Adi, 2.65-66)

Feeling pity upon these suffering souls, the devotees prayed to Lord Krishna for their deliverance.Sri Advaita Acharya, who is fifty years elder to Lord Chaitanya, was one such devotee.Sri Advaita was the combined incarnation of the potencies of Sada Shiva and Lord Mahavishnu.Seeing the people of the world completely immersed in material activities and suffer greatly the pangs of material miseries, Advaita Acharya became deeply pained at heart.Overwhelmed with compassion, He began teaching Bhagavad gita and Srimad Bhagavatam, by explaining their purports in accordance to the science of devotional service, and decrying the paths of philosophical speculation and fruitive activities.Srila Haridasa Thakura , Srivasa Pandita and several other elderly vaishnavas, regularly congregated at Advaita Prabhu's house and discussed the glories of the Supreme Lord together. Visvarupa, an expansion of Lord Balaram and the elder brother of Lord Chaitanya, was also among those who graced His audience.

gita bhagavata kahe acharya gosai

jnana-karma nindi kare bhaktira badai

(Chaitanya Caritamrta, Adi , 13.64)

Website - www.thegaudiyatreasuresofbengal.com

In Sri Chaitanya Mangala it has been recorded that the sad state of affairs of the entire world at that time, caused deep anguish within the heart of Narada muni, a close associate of the Supreme Lord.

Para dukhe katara narada mahamuni
Krishna-katha rasha-gaan dibasha rajani
Krishnakatha lobhe bule samsara bhramiya
Na shunila Krishna-nama jagata chahiya

(Chaitanya Mangala, Sutra Khanda, 2.27-28)

-

Sri Narada Muni, who always sang the nectarian pastimes of Lord Krishna day and night, felt deeply distressed observing the miseries of others. To give out the holy names of Sri Krishna, Narada muni wandered throughout the universe. But the people of this world, being too attached to their material possessions, were not eager to accept the holy names.

The great sage Narada could not hear the chanting of the holy names of Krishna, even after wandering throughout the entire world. He grew greatly astonished. He began thinking of ways and means of delivering the suffering people. Narada thought, "The venomous snake of Kali has bitten everyone and as a result, the people of this world are aflame and mesmerized by their illusory pride. Being solely devoted unto their genitals and belly, the people of this world have totally forgotten Krishna. Their heart is continuously afflicted with the poison of greed, fascination, lust, anger, intoxication, pride, and they needlessly live the philosophy of 'I' and 'mine'. But they cannot make out who they are and what is actually theirs".Seeing the miserable condition of the people in general in this age of Kali, the great sage Narada, became thoughtful and began considering. Finding no other way to rescue the people, Narada came wandering to the gates of Dwarka, the abode of the Supreme Lord.

Website - www.thegaudiyatreasuresofbengal.com

Aichhana lokera dukha dekhi mahamuni
Antare chintita haiya mone mone guni
Ghor kalikaale lokera na dekhi nistara
Bhromite bhromite gela Dwarkara daar

(Chaitanya Mangala, Sutra Khanda, 2.37-38)

Celestial pastimes - Lord Krishna's confidential revelations to Narada Muni :

Back in the spiritual world, Lord Krishna enquired from Narada muni regarding the cause of his sorrows. Narada muni expressed himself and answered," The songs celebrating Your exalted qualities are my nectarian foodstuffs. Hankering to preach Your glories, I traversed the world of birth and death. But I could not hear the chants of Your holy name traveling through the entire material world. Being absorbed in material activities, the people have forgotten You. Being intoxicated and enchanted with pride, the entire world has become devoid of Krishna. This is the cause of my sorrow. I see no means of delivering these (conditioned) people. This is the thought that keeps disturbing my mind". Hearing Narada's words, Lord Krishna smiled. He reminded Narada of an earlier vow He had made to devi Katyayani (Goddess Durga) about offering His Mahaprasadam and His causeless mercy unto all denizens of the material world. The Lord added that Rukmini devi had recently enlightened Him about the glories of pure devotional service unto Himself. Rukmini devi had previously revealed how the pure devotees forsake all of their interests, including attachment to their own existence, desire for liberation, etc for the sake of serving the Supreme Lord. One, who lives to drink and relish the nectar of the Lord's lotus feet, cares for neither day nor night nor any passing

Website - www.thegaudiyatreasuresofbengal.com

season. Hearing Rukmini devi's words, Lord Krishna had developed an unsatiated desire to taste the ecstatic bliss of His own love. This was something that bewildered even the Supreme Lord and He craved to experience this first hand, especially the deep ecstatic love that Srimati Radharani felt for Him. He wanted to understand how He was a reservoir of all sweetness and the attraction that drove His devotees crazy. Lord Krishna hence announced -

Bhunjibo Premar shukh, bhunjaibo loke
Deena bhab prakash kariba kaliyuge
Bhakata yanera sange bhakati kariya
Nija prema bilaiba isvara haiya

(Chaitanya Mangala, Sutrai, 2.101-102)

-

(Sri Krishna continued) 'I shall relish the bliss of My own ecstatic love, and I shall make the others taste this ecstasy as well. I shall manifest a form filled with humility in this kaliyuga. Along with the other devotees, I shall engage in devotional service and in the process ,I, the Supreme personality of Godhead, shall freely distribute the ecstatic love for Me to one and all'.

Nija guna sankirtana prakash kariba

Navadvipe Saci-grihe janama lobhibo
Gaura dirgha kalebara, bahu janu-sama
Sumeru sundara tanu ati anupama

(Chaitanya Mangala, Sutrai, 2.103-104)

-

'I shall manifest the congregational chanting of my glories. I shall take My birth at the house of Saci devi in Navadvipa. My body shall be fair *and long, with my arms reaching up to my knees. The matchless form of mine shall be as beautiful as Mount Sumeru'.*

Speaking thus, Lord Krishna manifested His form as Lord Gauranga beholding which Narada muni became overwhelmed with divine rapture. The form of the Lord was as glorious as Mount Sumeru and saturated with pure ecstatic love. Locana das writes in Sri Chaitanya Mangala that this was the first time that the form of Lord Gauranga had been manifest. Beholding the wonderful form of Lord Gauranga, Narada muni felt ecstatic in his heart. A thousand streams of tears gushed from his eyes. The beauty of the Lord resembled the radiance of millions of moons and He shone like a million of effulgent suns. His majestic form was as beautiful as millions of cupids combined together. Lord Krishna roared :

*Ghosona karoho shiva brahma adi loke
Gaura avatara muin haba Kaliyuge
Guna sankirtana nama prakash kariba*

Nija bhakti prema-rasa sukh prachariba

(Chaitanya Mangala, Sutrai, 2.113-114)

(Lord krishna continued) 'Announce at the residences of Shiva, Brahma, and all the other celestial planets, that I would advent as Lord Gauranga in the age of kali. I shall propagate the congregational chanting of My name and qualities. I shall preach the bliss of tasting the ecstatic love obtained by rendering devotional service unto Me'.

Sri Chaitanya Mangala records the confidential reasons behind Lord Gauranga's appearance.

*Shata shata shakha, bhaktipathe nahi shima
Ekmukh hauk lok, prachariba prema
Nija nija bhakta-jana ara parishad
Prithivi janam giya premabhakti swadh*

(Chaitanya Mangala, Sutrai, 2.115-116)

-

(Lord Krishna continued) "There are presently hundreds and hundreds of branches on the path of devotional service. There is no end to this. I would preach pure love unto the Supreme Lord and unite all these people.

Along with all my devotees and associates, I shall appear on earth. I shall relish the taste of ecstatic loving service unto Myself".

Biography of Chaitanya Mahaprabhu - In a nutshell :

Website - www.thegaudiyatreasuresofbengal.com

Sri Chaitanya Mahaprabhu's sublime pastimes are broadly classified into three phases- Adi Lila, Madhya Lila and Antya Lila. Of these, the pastimes classified under Adi lila ,spanning across the first 24 years of His life ,before He had accepted Sannyasa, were primarily enacted in the holy dham of Navadvipa.During these

Website - www.thegaudiyatreasuresofbengal.com

first 24 years,which encompasses the pastimes of Sri Gauranga's childhood (balya), early boyhood (Pauganda) ,later boyhood (Kaishore) and youth (yauvana), the Lord enchanted the pious residents of Navadvipa dham with His heart melting pastimes. It was during these years that the Lord had manifested the blissful pastimes of His marriage. The mesmerizing sankirtana pastimes at the house of His eternal associate ,Sri Srivasa Pandita, also occurred during this time.

It is only by the causeless mercy of the Supreme Lord that one gets the rare opportunity to gain entrance into this cintamani (spiritual) dham of Navadvipa and associate with its pious residents.This land is mingled with the dust of the Lord's lotus feet, and it is only by the blessings of our spiritual master and the mercy of Sri Gaurasundara, that we attempt to write a few lines in its glorification.

Lord Chaitanya, or Nimai as He was popularly known as, grew up to be a mischievous boy who would tease and taunt the other netizens. He would pick up fights and could not be defeated in any quarrel. Every day after finishing His studies at noon, Nimai would go and happily bathe in the holy Ganges. Countless people, including householders, sannyasis, distinguished gentlemen and children would accompany the Lord in these water pastimes. Nimai was an exceedingly intelligent student who could grasp His teacher, Gangadas Pandita's words, just by hearing them once. The other students became His followers simply by attending to His clever arguments. Navadvipa, being the seat of learning in those days, was full of educators. All of their students gathered in the Ganges after class and quarreled with each other. Nimai proceeded from one bathing Ghat to another, trying to find an audience of students with whom He could debate and argue. But no one could defeat the Lord when it came to debates. Going forward, Lord Chaitanya had debated with some of the most eminent Vedic scholars of His day - Kesava Kashmiri, Sarvabhauma Bhattacharya, and Prakashananda Sarasvati. The Lord was able to convince each one of them that the devotional service unto the Supreme Personality of God is superior to any other philosophical system.

After accepting the renounced order of life (Sannyasa), Lord Chaitanya left Navadvipa and shifted to Jagannatha Puri, where He spent the rest of His life. He had preached widely across India and inaugurated the sankirtana movement or the congregational chanting of the holy names of Lord Krishna.

Lord Chaitanya's Teachings in a Nutshell :

Sri Chaitanya Mahaprabhu had taught that we are not our bodies; instead we are spirit souls who are entrapped in these bodies of matter. In this precarious condition that we call life, we are actually striving to satisfy our innate spiritual desires while interacting with this world of matter through our material senses. The senses of our material body are prone to be attracted to matter. However our identity being spiritual, our satisfaction and fulfillment lies in interacting with the world of spirit. Sri Chaitanya Mahaprabhu explained that living entities are part and parcel of the Supreme Lord, the supreme spirit and it is his natural tendency to render selfless devotional service unto his

Website - www.thegaudiyatreasuresofbengal.com

eternal spiritual Lord. It is due to the absence or forgetfulness of this natural tendency to render selfless devotional service unto the Supreme Spirit, that the living entity gradually develops innumerable material hankerings by pursuing which or by enjoying which, a living entity foolishly thinks that he can obtain the unadulterated spiritual bliss that he had been searching throughout.

Hence a materialist who aspires to indulge or who indulges in gross material sense gratification has no escape from this quagmire of unending sensual desires which only serve in complicating his life and further deteriorates his consciousness.

He only ends up being frustrated though because he does not obtain what he has been originally and eternally searching for - which is unadulterated spiritual bliss which can be obtained only by rendering selfless devotional service.

Sri Chaitanya Mahaprabhu gave an analogy. He compared pure devotional service unto the supreme Lord to the all-illuminating sun while he compared one's service unto his own senses to the shadow. He explained that where there is sun there cannot be any shadows.

Krishna surya sama, maya haya andhakara,
Yahan Krishna, tahan nei mayara adhikara

Sri Chaitanya Mahaprabhu had instructed us to chant the Hare Krishna Mahamantra. This Hare Krishna Mahamantra finds its mention in the Kali santarana upanishad. It has been described as the supreme deliverer of the living entities in this day and age. Repeated chantings of this Hare Krishna Mahamantra cleanses the dust accumulated in our consciousness for millions and millions of lifetimes and helps evoke the essential spiritual emotions that form the very basis of our existence. By the mercy of Sri Chaitanya Mahaprabhu this Hare Krishna Mahamantra has spread all over the world today. The sixteen syllables of the 'Hare Krishna Mahamantra' which is the *'Hare Krishna Hare Krishna Krishna Krishna Hare Hare Hare Rama Hare Rama Rama Rama Hare Hare'* are not ordinary sound vibrations. They are fully endowed with the power and the qualities of the Supreme Lord. Regular chanting of this Hare Krishna mahamantra cleanses the impurities from our heart and helps bathe soul, body and mind in divine bliss. Mahaprabhu taught universal fraternity and inspired a spirit of brotherhood amongst devotees. Sri Chaitanya Mahaprabhu had taught that human thoughts should never be shackled with sectarian views. Sectarianism , by the way, is a product of one's own bodily conception of life. His teachings are universal and acceptable to all irrespective of one's ethnicity, race, culture, education, gender, etc.

Website - www.thegaudiyatreasuresofbengal.com

Chaitanya Mahaprabhu's causeless mercy :

Sri Chaitanya Mahaprabhu is the most munificent incarnation of the Supreme. He freely gives what no other incarnation of the Supreme Lord has ever given before - the ecstatic pure love of God. He does not consider one's qualifications or background or pedigree before bestowing this supreme gift upon them, receiving which one achieves the ultimate perfection of his human life. This ecstatic love of God eludes the great demigods like Brahma, Shiva and Indra. Even Lakshmi devi, the wife of Lord Narayana, hankers to receive it. A yogi cannot achieve it, even after performing severe austerities for thousands of years. A Jnani cannot smell it even after analysing the whole of the vedic scriptures. This ecstatic love of God is extremely rare but it can be easily achieved by the causeless mercy of Lord Gauranga. That is why lord Chaitanya is known to be the essence of all the other incarnations of the Supreme - 'Avatara sar Gaura avatara'.

Lord Narayana reveals this secret of all secrets to Devi Katyayani (Durga) :

Website - www.thegaudiyatreasuresofbengal.com

*E mor antara hiya, tomare kahila
iha
Sambari rakhoho nija mone
Saba avatara sar , Kali Gora
avatara
Nistariba lok nijagune
(Chaitanya Mangala, text 272)*

Translation -

(Lord Narayana continued) 'Now I have revealed my heart to you. Please keep this secret carefully locked away in your heart. Lord Gauranga, who shall appear in this age of kali, is the essence of all the other incarnations of the supreme. By the strength of His transcendental qualities, He shall deliver all people in Kali Yuga'.

That is why Sri Chaitanya Chandramrita states :

*Rakso-daitya-kulam hatam kiyad
idam yogadi-vartma-kriya-*

*Margo va prakati-kritah kiyad idam
sristy adhikam va kiyat*

Website - www.thegaudiyatreasuresofbengal.com

Mediny-uddharanadikam kiyad idam premojjvalaya maha-

Bhakter vartma-karim param bhagavatas Chaitanya-murtim stumah

(Chaitanya Chandramrita, Text 7)

-

What benefit did the world derive when the incarnations of the supreme Lord like Ramachandra, Nrsimha, and many others killed so many raksasa and Daityas ? What was the benefit derived when Lord kapila and other incarnations reveal the paths of sankhya and yoga ? Is it of great glory that Lord Brahma and other guna-avataras create, maintain and destroy the material universes ? How auspicious is it that Lord Varahadeva lifted and rescued the earth from the garbhodaka ocean ? We do not consider these pastimes to be so important. The most important of all things is that

Lord Chaitanya has revealed the great splendour of pure ecstatic love for Himself. Let us glorify that Lord Chaitanya Mahaprabhu.

Along with His associates, Sri Chaitanya Mahaprabhu has manifested the most blissful, heart rending pastimes that has ever been witnessed in human history. In fact, some of the eternal associates of the Lord have experienced a greater degree of transcendental ecstasy being part of the pastimes of Chaitanya Mahaprabhu, as compared to being part of Sri Krishna's vrindavana pastimes, as confirmed in the below verse.

Website - www.thegaudiyatreasuresofbengal.com

Ati aparupa leela prakashila prabhu

Chari yuge adbhut katha nahi shune kabhu

(Chaitanya Mangala , 1.94)

- Sri Chaitanya Mahaprabhu had manifested the most wonderful incomparable pastimes, never heard before in any of the four yugas.

Sri Chaitanya Chandramrita confirms that obtaining the causeless mercy of Lord Gauranga is the ultimate perfection in the life of a spiritual practitioner. He, who achieves it, hankers for nothing else in this entire creation. The heavenly abodes and the pursuits of liberation appear very insignificant to such a fortunate soul.

Kaivalyam narakayate tri dasa pur akasha puspayate

Durdantendriya kala sarpa patali protkhata damstrayate

Visvam purna sukhayate vidhi mahendradis ca kitayate

Yat karunya kataksa vaibhav-
avatam tam Gauram eva stumah

(Chaitanya Chandramrita, text 5)

-

For those who have attained the merciful sidelong glance of Sri Chaitanya Mahaprabhu, impersonal liberation (merging into the brahmajyoti) becomes as painful as going to hell, the heavenly cities of the demigods seem to be as trivial as mere flowers floating in the sky, the venomous and poisonous fangs of the untamable black snakes of the senses become extracted and uprooted, the whole world which is otherwise full of misery becomes full of supreme joy and the exalted positions of Brahma, Indra and all the demigods become as insignificant as those of tiny insects. Let us glorify that supremely merciful Lord Gauranga.

Gauranga Mora Dharma
(Gauranga is my 'dharma')

- *Composed by Srila Narahari Sarkara Thakura*

(Narahari Sarkara's Exclusive devotion unto Lord Chaitanya's lotus feet)

mana re! kaha na Gauranga katha

O mind, please constantly speak about the glories of Lord Gauranga (Chaitanya Mahaprabhu) !!! This is my advice to you.

**Gaurara nama amiyara dhama,
piriti murati data**

Gauranga's Holy Name is the supreme abode of all nectar and the personified bestower of unalloyed love and attachment to the supreme Lord.

**sayane Gaura svapane Gaura,
Gaura nayanera tara**

jivane gaura marane Gaura,
gaura galara hara

Remember Lord Gauranga while you are asleep, contemplate upon Him in Your dreams. He is the exclusive star and the vision of my eyes.

Gauranga is my life and I will hold onto Gauranga at the time of my death. gauranga is the priceless necklace that adorns my neck.

hiyara majhare Gauranga rakhiye, virale vasiya rabo
manera sadhete se rupa-candere, nayane nayane thobo

Keeping Gauranga within my heart ,I will relish His association sitting in a solitary place. Thus I will fix my mind on His supremely enchanting form and I will gaze into Lord Gauranga's exquisitely beautiful eyes.

Gaura vihane na vanchi parane,
Gaura korechi sara
Gaura boliya jauka jivane,
kichu na cahibo ara

Website - www.thegaudiyatreasuresofbengal.com

Without Gauranga's association I do not desire to maintain this body or live in this world. Lord Gauranga is the very essence of my existence. I wish to give up my life singing Lord Gauranga's name and glories-- I ask for nothing else in this world.

**Gaura gamana, Gaura gathana,
Gaura mukhera hamsi
Gaura-piriti, Gaura murati,
hiyaya rahalo pasi**

May Lord Gauranga's graceful movements, Lord Gauranga's splendid features and characteristics, Lord Gauranga's sweet smiling face, love and attachment for Lord Gauranga's glories and pastimes, and Lord Gauranga's nectarean delicate form - all of Them spontaneously enter and manifest in my heart at every moment

**Gauranga dharama, Gauranga karma,
Gauranga vedera sara
Gaura charane, parana samarpinu,
Gaura karibena para**

Worshiping Gauranga is my only Dharma or religion, Gauranga is the only object or goal of

Website - www.thegaudiyatreasuresofbengal.com

all my endeavours and Lord Gauranga's bhajana (loving worship) is the very essence of all the Vedic scriptures. I completely surrender my life, mind, body, heart and soul at Lord Gauranga's lotus feet. I am fully certain that Lord Gauranga shall deliver me from this great ocean of material existence.

**Gaura sabda Gaura sampada,
jahara hiyaya jage
narahari dasa tara carane,
sarana mage**

Gauranga's holy Name, form, glories and pastimes are the exclusive treasures for that fortunate person in whose heart Lord Gauranga manifests Himself by His causeless mercy. Narahari dasa prays and begs to be able to take shelter at the lotus feet of such an exalted devotee.

(Translated by Diptiman Gaurahari das & Diptimayi Vishnupriya devi dasi)

Website - www.thegaudiyatreasuresofbengal.com

Website - www.thegaudiyatreasuresofbengal.com

On a closing Note

Please visit our website for more such books and articles - https://www.thegaudiyatreasuresofbengal.com

We would love to hear back from you. Contact us - contact@thegaudiyatreasuresofbengal.com

Website - www.thegaudiyatreasuresofbengal.com

Made in the USA
Monee, IL
19 May 2022